Transprofessional Diplomacy

Transprofessional Diplomacy

By

Costas M. Constantinou, Noé Cornago,
and Fiona McConnell

BRILL

LEIDEN | BOSTON

Library of Congress Control Number: 2016958235

Typeface for the Latin, Greek, and Cyrillic scripts: "Brill". See and download: brill.com/brill-typeface.

ISBN 978-90-04-34044-2 (paperback)
ISBN 978-90-04-34072-5 (e-book)

Originally published as Volume 1(4) 2016, in *Diplomacy and Foreign Policy*, DOI 10.1163/24056006-12340005.

Published by Koninklijke Brill NV, Leiden, The Netherlands.
Koninklijke Brill NV incorporates the imprints Brill, Brill Hes & De Graaf, Brill Nijhoff, Brill Rodopi and Hotei Publishing.

Contents

Acknowledgements

The idea for this paper started in a productive exchange we had on this topic during an EISA Exploratory Symposium in Rapallo, Italy, 29 October–1 November 2014. We would like to thank the other participants of this Symposium (Corneliu Bjola, Sanderijn Duquet, Markus Kornprobst and Ole Jacob Sending) for their initial feedback. We would also like to thank the two anonymous reviewers for their very constructive comments.

Transprofessional Diplomacy

Costas M. Constantinou
University of Cyprus

Noé Cornago
University of the Basque Country (UPV/EHU)

Fiona McConnell
University of Oxford

Abstract

Diplomacy is no longer restricted to a single vocation nor implemented exclusively through interaction amongst official representatives. In exploring the challenges that these transformations produce, this work surveys firstly, the *genealogy* of diplomacy as a profession, tracing how it changed from a civic duty into a vocation requiring training and the acquisition of specific knowledge and skills. Secondly, using the lens of the *sociology* of professions, the development of diplomacy as a distinctive profession is examined, including its importance for the consolidation of the power of modern nation-states. Thirdly, it examines how the landscape of professional diplomacy is being diversified and enriched by a series of non-state actors, with their corresponding professionals, transforming the *phenomenology* of contemporary diplomacy. Rather than seeing this pluralization of diplomatic actors in negative terms as the *de*professionalization of diplomacy, we frame these trends as *trans*professionalization, that is, as a productive development that reflects the expanded diplomatic space and the intensified pace of global interconnections and networks, and the new possibilities they unleash for practising diplomacy in different milieus.

Keywords

diplomacy – diplomats – professions – professionalization – vocation – state – non-state – diplomatic skills – diplomatic innovation – diplomatic hybridity

 | DOI 10.1163/9789004340725_002

1 Introduction: Understanding Diplomatic Transformation through the Profession

> Professions are not only the bearers of knowledge; they are also, in effect, the secular guardians of the sacred, the priesthood of the modern world, but a priesthood which acknowledges the ultimate unknowability of things, deals in uncertainties, and recognizes the openness of the world to change. The professional system is the regulating system of the modern society, whose function is to accommodate society to this reality.
>
> DINGWALL AND KING 1995: 18

•••

> It is possible, of course, that the professional diplomat is an anomaly in democratic society and that we must seek new forms and procedures of foreign relations which are more fitting to this type of political community.
>
> CRAIG 1952: 158

∵

Beyond interstate and intergovernmental encounters, where else is diplomacy exercised today? Who can legitimately lay claim to be a practitioner of diplomacy, and how far is the distinction between professional and occasional diplomat helpful? To what extent is the profession of diplomacy changing, expanding, contracting or transformed beyond recognition? Such questions are not new, nor are they peculiar to the practice of diplomacy. They are especially topical under conditions of globalization and the increasing digitization of life, which have radically modified 'the realities of professional work' (Faulconbridge and Muzio 2012: 136). Professions are trying to catch up with these new realities. But as professional aspirations and expectations change, questions about the key qualities, skills and ethics of the profession are also posed anew. As are concerns about the loss of past mastery or the need to recalibrate 'professional' standards. In other words, a *professional* approach may be required to address the pressing needs and discharge the important tasks of modern life but also a *flexible professionalism* to meet the challenges of our changing work environment.

In diplomacy, as in other professions, objections concerning amateurish interventions and lack of professionalism are commonplace. As Harold Nicolson once protested: 'The art of diplomacy, as that of water-colours, has suffered much from the fascination which it exercises upon the amateur' (Nicolson, 1939: 54). Given that there is often more at stake in diplomatic failure than in the art of painting, this lament is both legitimate and urgent. This should not in any way be undervalued. Problems begin to appear, however, when claims to maintaining 'professional conduct' or a 'golden diplomatic standard', eschew democratic control and alternative diplomatic possibility.

Being a 'professional' diplomat is not necessarily equivalent to being a 'good' or a 'virtuous' diplomat. As Craig points out in the second epigram to this paper (1952: 158), one of the problematic features of professional diplomacy as developed in modern times is its considerable immunity to democratic scrutiny, such as in daily 'question time' before the Parliament. This is to a degree necessary and justifiable in not turning professional diplomats into professional politicians, whose job would simply become one of gratifying domestic audiences. Yet it comes at the price of partitioning responsibility and depoliticizing diplomacy, in itself a highly political activity. Moreover, diplomatic ontology has extended beyond the activities of the esteemed profession as we show below. To the extent that, nowadays, not only the state but a plethora of other glocal actors consciously exercise or claim to engage in diplomacy when managing their transnational relationships, such alternative reality will remain unacknowledged and indeed betrayed if we remain captives to a rather conservative understanding of the 'profession' and 'professionalism'.

In this paper, we focus on the profession not as 'secular guardians of the sacred' practice of diplomacy, but as curious witnesses recognizing 'the openness of the [diplomatic] world to change'. We suggest that the diplomatic profession, in the spirit of the two epigrams above, ought to be hospitable to new 'realities' and 'new forms and procedures of foreign relations'. This more flexible, accommodating approach to the profession we call *transprofessionalization*: a productive development that reflects the expanded diplomatic space and intensified pace of global interconnections and networks, and the new possibilities they unleash for practising diplomacy in different milieus. Put differently, we do not want to frame these new diplomatic trends negatively or casually as *deprofessionalization*, but rather to valorise them positively through association to other vocations and conscious daily performances that pertain to different types of diplomatic skill and engagement (see, for example, Constantinou, Kerr and Sharp 2016: 435–665). *Transprofessionalization* is thus an opening to the multiple worlds of diplomacy and the range of diplomatic 'migrations' across professions. But it also seeks to open up the study and understanding of diplomacy to the diverse *partnerships* and *hybridities* between national diplomatic services and a plethora of other professional actors as well as the 'non-professional' multitude.

Current transformations in diplomacy may be examined not only through its evolving practices and institutions but also through the prism of the radical changes affecting diplomacy as a profession (cfr. Rossow 1962; Harr 1969; Kennan 1997; Sharp 1997; Neumann 2005; Bazouni 2005; Niedner Kalthoff 2005, 2006). Diplomacy is no longer restricted to a single vocation; aspects of it can be found in different occupational positions. Former official diplomats are now increasingly active as international consultants at the service of both governments and companies (Riordan 2002; Ross 2007; Copeland 2009; Fletcher 2016). Governments also frequently hire former experienced activists, coming from the world of NGOs, hoping that their expertise will bring something new to their diplomatic performance in fields such as development and humanitarian aid (Lancaster 2008). Scientists increasingly have an influential voice in critical international negotiations in matters of technical complexity such as environmental governance (Princen 2007; Betsill and Corell 2008). Journalists, and creative industry and marketing specialists are behind the new interest in public diplomacy, national branding and digital diplomacy (Bjola and Holmes 2015). Meanwhile, global business consultants increasingly include diplomatic skills as one of the 'core' competences that corporate managers are required to master (cfr. Trice et al 1995; London 1999; Steger 2003; Muldoon 2005; Abbas 2009; Ordeix-Rigo and Duarte 2009) for better dealing with 'external pressures' in the global realm (cfr. Amann et al. 2011). This is not only in terms of their interactions with governments through its subsidiaries abroad, but also in a wider societal sense in terms of corporate interactions with stakeholders such as trade unions, NGOs, indigenous leaders, consumers and political parties (cfr. Saner et al. 2000).

Two particular trends in the changing relationship between diplomacy and professionalism are notable and will be examined in this paper. First, professional review boards (e.g. QDDR 2010; MAEDI 2015; Future FCO Report 2016) have outlined the need for developing *new skills, new methods and new partnerships* for the effective working of national and supranational diplomatic services which are tasked with the management of complex regional and global problems. In such a new context, new skills such as social media and digital literacy, transnational networking beyond traditional coalition building, remote sensing, data-mining, visual translation, Logical Framework Approach (LFA), Results Based Management (RBM), Right Based Programming (RBP), or information gathering through crowdsourcing, amongst other techniques, are becoming increasingly common in diplomatic practice (Bagger 2015). Second, the representation, networking and advocacy work of subnational, transnational and marginalized groups, as well as that of national institutions and governmental agencies not formally designated as 'diplomatic', suggests that sustained engagement with diplomatic practices has spread beyond the traditional diplomatic corps and cannot be credibly restricted to the foreign ministry officialdom. Whilst there is a clear demand for new professional skills for which traditional diplomats are not always well-equipped, outstanding professional achievements in delivering diplomatic excellence remain unrecognized or un-noticed in a context in which new forms of highly specialized expertise acquire a heightened importance.

In analyzing and addressing these challenges we first sketch out the historical context of diplomacy as a profession, tracing how it transformed from a civic duty into a vocation requiring training and the acquisition of specific knowledge and skills. We do this by outlining the depoliticization of diplomacy whereby it evolved from being a civic duty and 'occasional' vocation to a career and 'profession'. The latter is examined through the lens of Max Weber's work on the evolution of the professional politician whereby we attend to four key strata from which the diplomatic profession drew its personnel and vocational skills and mores: the clergy, the literati, the courtier and the jurist. Taking each in turn, we also trace how a number of well-known and influential treatises, generally written by experienced diplomats—such as Wicquefort and Callières—forged a 'weak' professional cannon for diplomats (cfr. Behrens 1936; Bazzoli 2001) which, despite the impact of the wider transformations experienced in world politics since the Congress of Vienna (Mösslang and Riotte 2008), remains recognizable even today (cfr. Satow 1917; Roberts 2010).

Having charted the historical institutionalisation of diplomacy through the creation of a professional 'establishment', our attention then turns to more recent pressures on professional diplomacy in the context of wider professional transformations vis-à-vis increasingly global demands of market forces and transnationalism. Using the lens of the *sociology* of professions we analyse how the development of diplomacy as a differentiated profession, important as it was for the consolidation of modern nation-states, produced nevertheless a rather paradoxical effect. The more specialized professional diplomats were, the more they became alienated from a variety of other professional worlds of paramount importance in shaping our contemporary world. This additionally explains why experienced professionals coming from a variety of domains—such as peace and development, human rights and political advocacy, business and corporate sectors, civil service, science and research, cultural organizations—are increasingly engaging in practices, strategies and indeed forums which had previously been deemed to be the exclusive domain of state diplomats. As such, we examine the extent to which the traditional barriers to entry in diplomacy are being broken down.

In the fourth section of the paper we examine how the landscape of professional diplomacy is being diversified and, we argue, enriched by a series of non-state actors. In the context of 'new diplomacy' (Cooper et al 2002; Riordan 2003) we chart the opening up of the diplomatic vocation to currently under-represented groups—e.g., NGOs (Betsill and Corell 2008) social movements (Keck and Sikkink 1998), minority communities (McConnell, et al 2012), sub-national governments (Kuznetsov 2014), and professionals whose diplomatic labour often remains under-appreciated such as everyday negotiators, mediators and peacemakers in conflict and crisis zones, community leaders and even celebrities (Cooper 2008). Rather than seeing this pluralization of diplomatic actors in negative terms as the *de*professionalization of diplomacy, we frame these trends as *trans*professionalization. In teasing apart the different dimensions of transprofessionalization we focus both on the 'new' skills and knowledges that non-state actors bring to the diplomatic realm and how non-state diplomats seek to 'learn the game' of diplomacy. We frame the former in terms of the functional specificity of the expertise and knowledge that non-state actors bring to transprofessional diplomacy, and the creative experimentation in diplomatic strategies that this facilitates. The latter is explored through the lenses of socialization and mimicry whereby these actors emulate, and in some cases subvert, formal diplomatic practices.

The paper concludes by summarising the arguments we have developed around the notion of transprofessionalization and indicating future research themes in this vein. We sketch out the idea of diplomatic partnerships and hybrid diplomacies as ways of framing the dynamic, collaborative and contingent nature of transprofessionalized diplomacy, and we point to ways that this concept can shape both the study and the practice of diplomacy.

2 Genealogy: The Professionalization of Diplomacy

A study of the professionalization of diplomacy should first entail an engagement with the notion of profession. It should also include an account of the sedimentation of professional claims as to skills exclusivity and expertise. How are we to understand professionalization processes as developed in Renaissance Europe? How are they linked to the diplomatic profession and other related vocations? To what extent do different claims about diplomatic skills inform different approaches to diplomatic theory and practice?

At the outset, two key meanings of profession have emerged from the Middle Ages and progressively modified in the Renaissance onwards. In the Middle Ages, the dominant view of profession was that of a public avowal, an affirmation of belonging to a religious order, a declaration 'professing an idea, a religious faith, a doctrine' (Biow 2002: 5). It was also used, however, in a more limited sense to cover the notion of a mental or manual occupation. In the Renaissance period, with the advent of secular and humanist culture, the latter meaning was enhanced while the former continued but progressively receded. That is to say, by way of acquiring a 'profession' it was no longer enough for someone *to declare to be something*, but rather one had *to make an effort to become something*.

Profession was thus associated with forms of 'art' and 'technique' and the kind of specialist knowledge that could be acquired and passed on in master-apprentice relationships. It became 'widely rooted in the growing rhetorical claims of professional identity and experience', through which individuals or groups of people empowered their daily avocations by 'professing knowledge of a subject' and thus indicating 'ability to perform certain tasks' vis-à-vis others' inability to discharge them, or discharge them as competently (Biow 2002: 6–7). Note, however, how this has had ambivalent implications. On the one hand, the 'professionalization' of a range of key occupations and public activities (e.g. doctors, lawyers, financers, secretaries, artisans), sought to mould ideal dispensers and train service providers. This upgraded the quality of their performance and was a clear positive development. On the other hand, those who came into the profession developed an interest in excluding the claims of those outside who also professed knowledge and ability to perform the same task. Inevitably, alternative service providers as practised in the quotidian and professing ability to perform outside the canon of official bodies became in effect 'amateurish' and 'unprofessional' and were side-lined.

To that extent, the professional 'establishment' has increasingly come to define the methods, tasks and goals of the vocation and indeed the limits within which it can be defined as one. As we discuss throughout this paper, crossing those limits and meddling with other professions, even though these may share similar methods, tasks and goals, tends to create unwelcome complications for the established practice and its study. Indeed an epistemological problem in the study of contemporary diplomacy which needs to be seriously engaged with, concerns how the 'profession' of diplomacy—in the sense of career diplomats of national diplomatic services—is consistently used in the field to decide what diplomacy is or can be (Der Derian 1987, Constantinou 1996, Sharp 2009, Cornago 2013). This has scholarly as well as practical implications and it is a point to which we return at the end of paper.

2.1 *Occasional and Professional Diplomacy*

To better understand the power shifts and ethical parameters of the professionalization of diplomacy, one needs to engage more broadly—historically as well as sociologically and politically—the idea of diplomacy as a vocation. Following on the footsteps of Max Weber's magisterial essay 'Politics as a Vocation', his distinction between 'occasional' and 'professional' politicians is highly useful in this regard (1991: 83–88). For our purposes, a similar distinction to Weber's can be drawn between 'occasional' and 'professional' diplomats.

As many scholars indicate, diplomacy is a historical human avocation—be it in the form of representing the positions, negotiating the interests, or mediating the differences between two or more 'sides' or political communities, and even used derogatorily as an elite, decadent occupation (e.g. Numelin 1960, Der Derian 1987, Black 2010, Leira 2016). Such diplomatic pursuits can be said to be 'occasional' when practised only as the need arises and sometimes while in the process of exercising other vocations. To the extent of not being a permanent occupation, diplomacy therefore features as a *minor* vocation. However, when one is wholly and/or exclusively dedicated to diplomatic pursuits then it can be said to practise diplomacy as a *major* vocation. To follow Weber's rationale for the political vocation, the latter basically means that one lives 'for' diplomacy or 'off' diplomacy or both. *Living for diplomacy*, in the sense of deriving life meaning from one's diplomatic service; *living off diplomacy*, in the sense of deriving economic benefit and income from such service. In a nutshell, the professionalization of diplomacy entails this living for and/or off its practice and how in this regard diplomacy has been historically evolved from a minor into a major human vocation.

What have been the implications of this professionalization of diplomacy? Firstly, and quite crucially, it brought about a *depoliticization* of diplomacy, as it was no longer viewed as a *civic duty* but on the contrary progressively as a *career*. Historically and prior to professionalization, being elected as a diplomat by the polis or selected by the prince was always a prestigious position. One derived much symbolic status and political capital from it. The chosen one could be sent alone or in a collective embassy with other ambassadors, but there was no service payment and one was not supposed to derive any economic benefit from discharging one's diplomatic duty (Mattingly 1988). In ancient Greece and Rome, free citizenship was supported by a slave economy, which literally freed citizens to be absent for long periods abroad in pursuit of their diplomatic avocations, including ecumenical embassies to survey the world and be informed about the laws and customs of other people (Constantinou 1996 and 2013). Similarly, in medieval Europe ambassadors had to be of financial means, typically nobles or holders of feudal estates; not only were they not paid, apart from a small stipend, but they often had to cover their own expenses. In fact a lot of diplomatic communication concerned out of pocket expenses when the embassy was delayed (Mattingly 1988: 31). In addition, there was considerable *risk taking* in becoming an ambassador in a period where diplomatic immunity was not absolute but conditional on diplomatic conduct while in foreign courts (Frey and Frey 1999). Finally there was considerable functional *responsibility* that ambassadors had to uphold, given that they were liable directly to their own polity, the assembly or the principal that assigned them on a mission. In short, the historical diplomatic vocation came with occupational hazards as well as extensive political responsibilities. These liabilities and responsibilities progressively shifted following professionalization.

One of the earliest examples of testing the limits of diplomatic responsibility was the classic trial of Aeschines in Athens on the charge of 'parapresbeia' (false embassy) in the 4th century BCE. The charge was made by Demosthenes, a famous orator but also co-ambassador of Aeschines in the Athenian embassy to the Macedonians, specifically on the alleged misconduct of diplomatic duties. These duties were specifically outlined as: (a) faithful execution of instructions; (b) faithful reporting on mission; (c) appropriate ambassadorial conduct; (d) taking advantage of time and opportunities; and (e) sound advice with regard to policy formulation. In Demosthenes' oration (2000) and Aeschines' response (2005) the contours of what constitutes faithfulness, appropriateness, opportunity and good advice are hotly debated as expected in such public trials. Whilst (a), (b) and (c) can be equally and easily found in codes of 'professional' responsibility nowadays, (d) and (e) are not likely to be found. By contrast, sound advice and not losing opportunities are viewed as 'political' responsibility for which a career diplomat would not be expected to be publicly questioned or go to trial for. Nor would a politician go to trial for that matter, although s/he might lose the next election. In other words, at the outset, there is considerable loss of responsibility in 'professionally' practising diplomacy in current times. Diplomacy as an 'occasional' vocation in those times was a more politically demanding business vis-à-vis the limited responsibility of 'professional' state diplomats nowadays.

With regard to European practice, the need for 'permanent representation' and 'continuous negotiation' has had implications in terms of professional practice. The rise of the resident embassy during the Renaissance period is viewed as the key innovation underscoring the shift from 'occasional' to 'permanent' diplomatic vocation. Ambassadors were sent to reside abroad for quite long periods of time, and thus fully immersed in foreign cultures. While abroad they participated in court life, observed and got to know the political protagonists of the country, and provided a constant flow of information to their state on the basis of which policy was developed or revised (Mattingly 1988: 87–102). As they were now permanently living abroad and permanently engaged in the diplomatic vocation, they were increasingly not able to practise other vocations in parallel to the diplomatic one. This is when, in Weberian terms, they started living for and off diplomacy.

Professional living for and off diplomacy notwithstanding, François de Callières in *On The Manner of Negotiating with Sovereign Princes* (1716/1983) would still lament the lack of professionalism and training in diplomacy, quite unlike that 'acquired by the profession of arms' (Callières 1983: 66). Callières protests how for an 'employ so difficult to be discharged as this' there is lack of a single 'discipline, or certain rules, established for training fit persons in the knowledge of such things as are necessary for those sorts of employments' (Ibid.). For him diplomacy is not a vocation that can be discharged through heroic adventurous moves. Callières suggests that quite often 'the science of treating and negotiating' ends up being undertaken suddenly by political novices or 'men of very indifferent talents' who end up being 'intoxicated with the honours' of the office. These appointed diplomats lack professionalism and simply function as 'heralds rather than ambassadors' proclaiming the greatness of their master but incapable of productive engagement and successful negotiation of agreements (Callières 1983: 66–7).

2.2 *Vocational Resources of the Diplomatic Profession*

Turning to focus more squarely on diplomacy as a profession it is useful to remain with Max Weber's frameworks. Weber views the evolution of the *professional politician* as being the result of a struggle for the centralization of power. Specifically, it entailed the gathering of support for the prince and his policies over a given territory vis-à-vis the local authority that was exercised by feudal lords in their estates. Weber provides an overview of the 'major types of these professional politicians' (1991: 92), which we can also utilize in the context of the *professional diplomat*, whilst also registering and appreciating differences. We shall concentrate on four strata from which the diplomatic profession drew its major source: (1) the clergy, (2) the literati, (3) the courtier, and (4) the jurist.

2.2.1 The Clergy

The Renaissance prince used the clergy to gather political support mainly for three reasons. First, as with other groups discussed below, the clergy were amongst the 'politically exploitable strata outside of the order of the estates'; second, they were literate and wielded authority against the aristocracy; third, communal life and clerical celibacy (where applicable) set them 'outside the machinery of normal political and economic interests' associated with family estates and private pursuits (Weber 1991: 92). In this regard, Weber sees similar patterns in the employment of the clergy in the politics of Medieval Europe, pre-colonized India, China and Japan. Although Weber does not expand on the specific role of the clergy in diplomacy, we know from diplomatic scholars that their counseling and representation capacity certainly extended to diplomatic practice.

In the context of European diplomacy, there was an additional reason for employing the clergy in diplomatic work; specifically, the central role that the Pope had in medieval and early renaissance diplomacy. Mattingly suggests that before the mid-16th century 'ecclesiastics had been rather commoner as ambassadors than laymen' but towards the end of the century, with the advent of Reformation and Counter-Reformation, their allegiance began to be seriously questioned (Mattingly 1988: 185–6). Writing in the mid-17th century, Cardinal Richelieu explains the utility of *continuous negotiation* with everyone and how 'it is necessary to act everywhere, near and far, and above all in Rome ... which has long been the diplomatic and geographical centre of the world' (Richelieu 1961: 95–96). Morevoer, speaking of the choice of ministers sent to negotiate with sovereign princes in the early 18th century, Callières sees the value of sending ecclesiastics (Cardinals or Bishops) to Rome. However, in view of the divided loyalties that the ecclesiastics may have between their nation and the Pope, he strongly advises that they are sent as assistants to ambassadors who will defend national interests with more vigour (1983: 167). In a nutshell, Callières sees the wider and significant diplomatic role that a cardinal, an abbot, a monk or a friar can play, 'rendering important services to the State', if he effectively ceases to practise his religious vocation and 'give himself up wholly to the affairs of his Prince.' (Callières 1983: 168).

From this perspective, the most celebrated example in modern European diplomatic history has been Cardinal Richelieu. Richelieu initially opted for a military career but had to abandon it in order to fulfill a vacant bishopric claim that was linked to his family. His theological studies and canonical preparation helped him get acquainted with the court of Rome. Subsequently as the representative of the clergy to the Estates General, his impressive advisory and mediatory ability won him royal favour, and he became French Secretary of State in 1614. Most notable during his reign is the application of the principle of raison d'état, by which Richelieu bypassed theological considerations and initiated policies that he judged to be in the French national interest. Thus France joined the Protestant side during the Thirty Years War and against the Holy Roman Emperor and Catholic States. Henry Kissinger, among others, viewed Richelieu as the pioneering figure of modern diplomacy, who transcended 'the essential pieties of his age' and did not allow 'his vocation as cardinal' to misconceive 'the Habsburg attempt to re-establish the Catholic religion' as anything other than a 'political maneuver' and 'geopolitical threat' (Kissinger 1994: 58–59). In Richelieu's example, therefore, the ecclesiastical vocation becomes fully subservient and instrumentally transferred to the diplomatic one.

A key advantage of the clergy as well as the theologians in pursuing the diplomatic vocation was their knowledge and capacity to employ religious discourse in their everyday work. This was especially important in the European diplomatic context, which was only partially and slowly secularized following the Renaissance. Worldwide, the work of missionaries was directly or indirectly coopted to complete the colonial diplomatic project but also to provide counter-colonial rationales, such as in liberation theology in Latin America and Sub-Saharan Africa (Opondo 2016). Moreover, with regard to the legitimation of global diplomatic pursuits and territorial expansion in the 'new world', the role of theologician-jurists like Vitoria and Suarez are highly important, with regard to de-legitimizing the universal empire claims that were subcontracted by the Pope, while framing more 'rational' and 'moral' principles that legitimized the policies of European empires (Behr 2010). In short, the clergy and theologically informed scholars were useful to the diplomatic profession to the extent that they were willing to transfer their allegiance to emerging secular powers and/or acted as mediators between them and religious authorities.

2.2.2 The Literati

The second major vocation that Weber identifies as the source of the professional politician are 'the humanistically educated literati', helping the ruler produce a more refined speech, becoming his advisor and acting as memorialists of key events (Weber 1991: 92). Yet during the Renaissance the diplomatic profession is linked to the humanist endeavour in more pronounced ways than the political profession. The humanist task involved a venture to know the world beyond religious universalism, dilettantism or limited local knowledge and this strongly associated humanist scholarship with the diplomatic mission (Constantinou 2013). For Max Weber, diplomacy becomes 'a *consciously* cultivated art' whose aficionados 'were in the main educated humanistically' and 'treated one another as trained initiates' (Weber 1991: 89). Diplomatic writers and practitioners, such as the Venetian Ermolao Barbaro and Ottaviano Maggi, very much saw the diplomatic vocation taking place in parallel to humanist endeavours. Both had 'a shared vision of the resident ambassador as a tireless, self-sacrificing participant' working abroad 'for the good of the state' (Biow 2002: 20–21). Furthermore, Maggi who 'idealizes the profession' does so through such classical models as Odysseus, symbolizing the worldly wisdom and resourcefulness acquired through tireless voyaging and adventure (Ibid.). It is through such experiences, not just deep and intense study, that diplomatic prudence is cultivated. As Maggi explains:

> But since prudence itself is a certain state of mind by which, by means of a certain reasoning, we have the choice of good and bad things; or rather it is refined knowledge of those things that must be sought or fled, and which pertain to public workings and the life of men, it seems that is acquired foremost from experience of affairs ... especially by the example of others, men in time become prudent, we want our ambassador to have obtained that example from travel, in which he has spent much time ... wisdom does not get enough help from reading, unless practice in handling affairs comes to it in addition.
>
> MAGGI QUOTED IN BIOW 2002: 124–125

Where the question of 'the ideal ambassador' is posed in a sustained way, one of the key skills suggested for diplomats is erudition. As outlined by Maggi, diplomatic knowledge is not just philosophical or academic, but deeply ingrained in experiential knowledge. Also, the possession of great knowledge is not viewed as mere courtly embellishment, aiming to impress nobility and symbolically elevate the diplomat before foreign audiences, though the latter is also necessary as shown below. Erudition is an occupational necessity, viewed as broad awareness combined with knowledge of minor differences which is seasoned by experience; that is, practical knowledge of the world and those 'significant others' with whom one needs to engage on a daily basis.

The notion of practising diplomacy through travelling and extending the horizons of knowledge stems from the early association of diplomacy with *theoria* in ancient Greece, which reveals the diplomatic vocation as a proto-philosophical occupation. Theoria was the name for the solemn-sacred embassy sent to consult the oracle as well as the ecumenical embassy discharged to see the world and bring back knowledge to the polis from abroad. Clearly this has the Odyssean sense of venture and ceaseless pursuit, but also the acquaintance and comparative assessment of different value systems, including one's own, as a means of instrumentally or constructively relating to others (Constantinou 1996 and 2006).

It is from this perspective that one realizes how diplomatic knowledge cannot be restricted to the mere strategic information and intelligence acquired by spies, even though the diplomat has been dubbed an 'honourable spy' precisely because that kind of knowledge was also required. Diplomatic knowledge about others required an anthropological insight, offering nuanced perspectives and understandings that were not available to the uninitiated. The Venetian *relazioni* was perhaps the best example of a diplomatic report that was a comprehensive scholarly reflection and advisory essay on the relation between Venice and other city-states, that not only informed but could serve as the beginning of a debate about policy (Bowd 2000; cfr. Queller 1967). Diplomatic knowledge was also the result of co-production; it linked to the personal experience that diplomats acquired by living abroad and dealing with others as well as the accumulated knowledge that was written down, archived and studied in universities (Cornago 2016).

Callières argues that worldly knowledge, humanist or courtly, is necessary but not a sufficient condition for undertaking the diplomatic profession. For him diplomatic knowledge also requires disciplined schooling, training and development. This kind of training started through Diplomatic Academies in the 18th century initially in France, Spain and the Holy See. Yet as Rossow argues professionalization did not immediately strike root but rather 'started hesitantly and gradually at the end of the Napoleonic wars, as diplomacy began to be conceived less as a mannered art of courtly intrigue and more as a field requiring experience, skill, and broader horizons' (Rossow 1962: 563).

With regard to diplomatic knowledge, high expectations and idealizations of polymathy characterize early Renaissance diplomatic writers. As Garrett Mattingly puts it, some writers, like Ottaviano Maggi, 'scarcely omitted anything from what an ambassador should know', including:

> First of all, theology and sacred letters. Then all branches of secular knowledge: mathematics, including architecture and mechanical drawing, music, geometry, astronomy. The whole of philosophy, natural and moral, including, of course, a special mastery of the civil and the canon law, as well as of the municipal law and statutes both of his own country and of that to which he was assigned.
>
> MATTINGLY, 1955: 186

This is in addition to being 'deeply read in literature and eloquent in the Latin tongue', as well as all the principal languages (Ibid.). Exaggerated demands, perhaps, though quite revealing of the wider humanist culture and of the need to get to know the world beyond the mono-religious dogmatism of medieval times. While aiming high, Antoine Pecquet still challenged the pansophic and multi-skilled vision of the diplomat. He realized human limitations in skills acquisition and the practical problem of idealization and so suggested that a division of diplomatic labour was necessary:

> If a single man could embody all the qualities of heart and spirit and the external advantages which have just been mentioned [of the ideal ambassador], he would be suitable for all countries, and for all kinds of business. But, as has already been said, one should not hope for this; in fact, there are no persons who do not differ in some ways from the general picture that one believed it necessary to paint. No two issues are identical, just as no two nations of the world, and no two governments have exactly the same character. So that no one man can be suitable for every situation everywhere, however gifted with excellent qualities.
>
> PECQUET 1737/2004: 164–5

Writing in the 18th century, Pecquet was implicitly criticizing the idealizations of the courtier-diplomat, who was elevated through his symbolic displays of high knowledge and ability to exercise mannered behaviour and to negotiate on every issue.

2.2.3 The Courtier

Whereas the humanist literati had much influence over the political—and indeed the diplomatic—vocation in the 16th century, Weber suggests that by the 17th century the court nobility had started to displace them. As part of consolidating their power, the princes 'drew the noble to the court and used them in their political and diplomatic service' (Weber 1991: 93). The vocation of the courtier had become instrumental for the practice of diplomacy because of shifts in the sites of its operation. The popular theatre that accompanied the pageantry of the ambassadorial entry in the Middles Ages and early Renaissance was progressively substituted by the more eclectic and refined theatre of the court as performed before the local nobility and resident diplomatic corps in European capitals (Mattingly 1988: 207). Although the theatrical aspect of diplomacy is not a Renaissance innovation, and historically linked to visual forms of communicating political meaning (Constantinou 1996: 95–120), it is in the Renaissance court that the theatrical diplomat perfects his art. This is also the time that the courtier and the prince begin to view their performativity as fully instrumental to the diplomatic vocation.

The classic work on court behaviour, written in the 16th century, is Baldassar Castiglione's *The Book of the Courtier*. Castiglione served himself as a diplomat, but his book is actually an account of courtiership as a new profession, as mentioned in his Letters:

> Among the other things that have come about in recent times, beyond which we have no news of, we see now emerging this sort of man that

> we call the courtier, a profession [*professione*] quite widely exercised throughout all Christendom ... only recently has a profession been made of this court service, if we can call it that, only recently has it been refined to an art and a discipline.
>
> QUOTED IN BIOW 2002: 10

In this profession, serving the princes and great lords, some courtiers are favoured because of 'valor in arms', others for 'knowledge of letters', others for 'physical beauty' and yet others 'for none of these reasons but only for a certain hidden conformity of their nature' (Ibid.). Castiglione proceeds with a vivid description of fictional conversations between court members, where the qualities of the warrior, the scholar and the faithful person are invariably projected into the perfect courtier who is thus effectively presented as the successor to the medieval knight. To that extent, the 'preoccupation with social distinction and outward forms of polite behaviour' conceals 'the most shameless opportunism under the cloak of tiresome refinement' of language and mannerism and that is itself elevated into a work of art (Bull's introduction in Castiglione 1976: 15 and 17). Castiglione provides detailed accounts of how to perfect courtiership through careful self-praise as well as praising others, the cultivation of looks and appearance, the acquisition of graceful movements and gestures, employing elegant and tactful writing and speaking, modestly responding to favours and honours, concealing or faking ignorance, displaying dignity, eloquence and wit, enticing laughter, and generally aiming to please (Castiglione 1976: 59, 61, 65, 77–80, 93, 127, 147, 149, 150–2, 155, 265).

For Castiglione, the courtier avoids affectation by practicing the art of nonchalance (*sprezzatura*). It is the most duplicitous art, because it is *the art of concealing art*.

> I have discovered a universal rule which seems to apply more than any other in all human actions or words: namely, to steer away from affectation at all costs, as if it were a rough and dangerous reef (to use perhaps a novel word for it) to practise in all things a certain nonchalance which conceals all artistry and makes whatever one says or does seem uncontrived and effortless.
>
> CASTIGLIONE 1976: 67

For Castiglione 'true art is what does not seem to be art' (Ibid.) and court life requires such duplicitous appearance. One cannot simulate knowledge of everything. Indeed one must, as in court masquerade, play the part that 'he feels himself best, to bring out its most important elements with diligence and elegance, while showing a certain nonchalance with regard to what is not essential' (Castiglione 1976: 119). Unlike the literarti who are expected to be fully immersed in the new renaissance knowledge, the courtiers practice *ludic humanism* and become *posers of knowledge and civility*.

Their behavioural comedy is perhaps what leads Wicqeufort to suggest that 'in the whole commerce of the world there is not a more comical personage than the ambassador' and that 'there is not a more illustrious theatre than a court'. But Wicquefort continues that it is crucial for the ambassador after that part is well played and the curtain is drawn, to 'cease to act the comedian' and instead start acting with honour and dignity (Wicquefort 2004: 129). In other words, it would be wrong to simply view courtiership as play-acting and as lacking functionality and purpose. Indeed, it can be seen as part of learning to practice what Bernard du Rosier identified in *Ambaxiator Brevilogus* (1436) as *equanimitas*—even-temperedness. In effect, a 'civilizing of emotions', which seeks to differentiate feeling from responses, ban verbal outbursts as unprofessional and thus enhance predictability in negotiations and diplomatic encounters (Masternbrock 1999). An approach that for some elevates the ideal professional diplomat not as a mere virtuous practitioner in the courts of states but as a 'courtier of civilization' (Sofer 2013).

2.2.4 The Jurist

For Weber, the most important stratum supporting professional politics is the 'universally-trained jurist' as developed in the Occidental 'political structure' and for which 'there is no analogy to this process to be found in any area of the world' (1991: 93). This is not to say that 'rational juristic thinking' has not been cultivated in non-European contexts. Rather, it denotes how unlike other places that were not under the legacy of Roman law, in the Occident the trained jurist retained autonomy from religious jurisprudence. This kind of juristic thinking concentrated on the production of legal arguments through the rationalization of legal opinions, submissions and trial procedures (Weber 1991: 93–94). This notion of professional advocacy has also influenced diplomacy, especially in the way it developed beyond the traditional skills linked to the ancient Greek and Roman oration.

The need of the advocate in both politics and diplomacy has to do with the ability of the trained lawyer 'to plead effectively the cause of interested officials ... win a cause supported by logically weak arguments and one which, in this sense, is a "weak" cause' (1991: 94). Even though Weber does not explicitly deal with the diplomat in this context, one might see the advocacy function of the professional diplomat as being somewhere in-between the 'genuine official' and the 'professional politician'. The genuine official is not supposed to engage in politics and practices his vocation *sine ira et studio*—i.e. without scorn and bias; the professional politician must fight with words, take a stand and display passion in defence of his cause (Weber 1991: 95). Diplomatic scholars broadly agree, however, that the diplomat ought to vigorously defend and promote the cause of his master yet this should be done without scorn and bias, and indeed combined with a deliberate attempt to include into one's understanding and discourse, the passions and biases of the other side:

> He must subdue his own feelings to get in place of the Prince with whom he deals, he transforms himself, so as to speak in him, he enters himself in his opinions and inclinations after having known him, and asks himself, as if in the place of the Prince with the same power, the same passions, and the same prejudices, what effects do these ways of representing him produce in me.
>
> CALLIÈRES QUOTED IN SATOW 1917: 134

In practice, this call to subdue one's feelings may function either as instrumental empathy or camouflaged injunction to know the other side so as to defeat its cause. Although the diplomatic vocation employs rational juristic thinking there are also clear diversions in its practice vis-à-vis the legal vocation. Like the legal vocation it is often in the business of interested advocacy, selectively employing supporting data like past agreements, customary rules, moral edicts and historical precedents in order to build a case for one's side. In producing one-sided arguments, however, one must imagine the counter-arguments, and be willing to synthesize negotiated settlements.

Familiarity and training in the proper use of such supporting data was a major concern for European diplomacy since the early 18th century and was combined with the establishment of Political Academies charged with training diplomats in the art of negotiation. The establishment of a *depot* of official documents in the French Political Academy was of paramount importance and a major step in this direction: on the one hand, centralizing and classifying documents that the Foreign Ministry needed, and, on the other hand, providing a resource of historical precedents which could be studied and reflected upon with regard to usage. Very influential in the French Political Academy, at least in the initial stages of its creation, were not the ambassadors and negotiators, but rather the secretaries, archivists and bibliophiles, who were 'more experienced it would be true to say in diplomatics than in diplomacy' (Keens-Soper 1983: 194). Beyond acquaintance with legal-historical precedent, diplomatics—the study of the form and content of ancient diplomas—served in training 'diplomats' in understanding historical forms of composition, changes in writing styles, euphemism, ambiguity, loopholes and so on, all important in the development of diplomatic drafting and 'double hand' crafting (Constantinou 1996:

69–89). It thus went beyond the art of the advocate or ancient orator of arguing a cause, and into the scriptural crafting of meaning that pre-formed and in-formed negotiation. Schweizer explains Callières' thinking in this regard:

> Throughout [Callières] emphasized the importance of compositional accuracy and style in the drafting of diplomatic instructions, official dispatches, treaties, and other related communiques. Emphasizing the connections between literary form in its many sidedness and the expository dimensions of the diplomatic art, Callières realized that political perception and literary expression were symbiotically related, combining elements at once descriptive and analytical from which important insights into the essential principles of effective negotiation can be distilled.
>
> SCHWEIZER 2011: 621

In Callières' thinking, the diplomatic profession of the 18th century begins to borrow from the profession of the secretary that was idealized by Tasso in the 16th century. According to Tasso, the crucial difference between the secretary and the diplomat-orator or advocate is that the secretary practises 'tacit persuasion'. Although in some respects, the profession of the secretary is analogous to that of the orator—'the art of writing letters is very similar to that of writing orations'—quite unlike the orator, the secretary is not into the business of passionate talk or flashy writing: 'what is acceptable in the oration would be overbearing in a letter' (Tasso quoted in Biow 2002: 188–189). Thus the secretary 'does not live among the schools of rhetors or of the sophists' for 'the orator reigns among judges, as one sees in our times in Venice; but the action of the secretary is very far away from the noises of the palace and of the battling of litigants' (Ibid., 188, 190). For Tasso, there is a spatio-temporal distinction between the orator and the secretary that needs to be recognized: 'the orator speaks to those present, the secretary to those far away' (Ibid., 188).

Yet, it is important to note that the secretary is not just a letter-writer; he 'takes his name from silence' and paradoxically persuades tacitly through this 'rhetoric of silence', in elliptical and implicit ways (Biow 2002: 190). It is at this point that the differences between the orator-advocate and the diplomat that 18th centrury diplomatic theorists began to imagine can be fully appreciated. The importance of advocating for a cause or seeking settlement through discretion, devaluation and understatement is valued more highly than intense valorisation and overstatement. Tasso refers to how the secretary achieves tacit persuasion through *disprezzo* (devaluing), by writing in a way that implies 'that there exists a vast reservoir of untouched speech and meaning' (Ibid., 190–191). This very noble profession of the secretary—which for Tasso writing in the 16th century was superior to the 'second place' of the ambassador (Ibid., 189)—the diplomatic profession sought to emulate and develop through the scriptural care, compositional accuracy and ultimately 'professional' drafting of treaties, dispatches and memoranda.

2.3 *A 'Weak' Profession?*

Overall the professionalization of diplomacy has been a long historical process, which has severed diplomacy from the sense of being a civic duty, turning it into a high profile and often well-paid career. In servicing the prince or the state, and in line with the political vocation, the diplomatic profession primarily emphasized an ethic of ultimate ends (Weber 1991: 120–127), also popularized in diplomacy as an ethic of *raison d'état* (Richelieu 1961, Kissinger 1994). But it did not ignore, and in fact had to cultivate, an ethic of responsibility to the wider society of states, also known as *raison de système* (see Watson 1984, Wiseman 2005, Sharp 2009). In other words, as a vocation, diplomacy had to pursue national and nationalist ends, while always taking into account the international contexts and cosmopolitan environments within which diplomacy operated. As we discuss below, this transnational dimension of the profession sets it apart from many other vocations that have only been transformed more recently, i.e. following the mobilities and opportunities of globalization.

The professionalization of diplomacy has historically borrowed from different vocations as outlined above. But it has not established anything close to a strict professional canon. In fact, it could be said that its professionalization has been 'weak' or 'incomplete'. This is something that is still lamented by long-serving and high profile diplomats, such as Freeman (1995: n.p.), who concludes that 'diplomacy does have all of the attributes of a profession, but that they remain in inchoate form'. A major reason for this has been the fact that, notwithstanding the sustained diplomatic training that career diplomats began to receive in major national diplomatic services in Europe from the 18th century onwards, one could still become a practitioner through political appointment—be it an ad hoc diplomat or a permanent ambassador or even a foreign minister—without any vocational training whatsoever. A head of state or government might have had some key diplomatic qualities of the appointee in mind when making such appointments, but of course other considerations were also at play. Yet, broadly speaking, three sets of skills seem to have endured from the treatises of diplomatic scholars: *firstly*, skills in the deep and nuanced knowledge of others with whom one related or managed relations with; *secondly*, skills in advocacy, composing arguments and defending/promoting a case; and *thirdly* skills in maintaining composure and working relationships which could be translated into attaining objectives and negotiating agreements.

Implementing these skills can lead to a rather broad professional remit. As Canadian diplomat and philosopher De Raymond (2015) contends, beyond representing the particular, the most important mission of the diplomat is to discover the universal in the particular and, correspondingly, the particular in the universal. Aware of the global risks affecting humanity, his thesis enhances a holistic, soul-searching approach focusing not just on the moblization of means and key skills but the pursuit of global ends (De Raymond 2015: 352–356). Yet reflecting on 'diplomacy as a profession' in the 1960s, the famous US diplomat George Kennan argued that '[d]iplomacy is a profession which until recently had never fully found its own soul or discovered its own proper dignity' (Kennan 2015). This was blamed by Kennan on the fact it was a profession of the high society, promoting a life remote from the people it was meant to serve, applying its skills of 'accuracy, imagination, tact and good sense' only with regard to 'a small group of highly placed and influential individuals'. To overcome the frustrations and loneliness of diplomatic work, he suggested the profession to be approached as 'a way of life':

> One must be able to love the great diversity of nature and of human living—to forget one's self at times, to be curious and detached and observant, to be sensitive to beauty and to tragedy, grateful for the opportunity to see life from many sides, accepting gladly the challenge that the external world presents to the understanding and the capacity for wonder.
>
> KENNAN 2015: N.P.

Even though Kennan would probably not have agreed with the transprofessionalization thesis put forward in our paper, we suggest that it is precisely this kind of insight that sensitizes us into the issues of the profession and recognizes diplomacy's transferable skills in understanding and negotiating the 'great diversity of nature and of human living'.

3 Sociology: Diplomacy as a Distinctive and Paradoxical Profession

In our examination of the transformations of diplomacy through those of its profession, thus far we have charted the historical institutionalization of diplomacy which created a professional 'establishment', that formed and sought to police the boundaries of the profession as defined by its practices, strategies and goals. The more specialized professional diplomats were, the more they became alienated from a variety of other professional worlds of paramount importance in shaping contemporary global life, thus becoming increasingly exclusionary. This additionally explains why experienced professionals coming from a variety of domains—such as peace and development, human rights and political advocacy, business and corporate sectors, civil service, science and research, and culture and the arts—are becoming increasingly involved in international activities, reacting in a way to that exclusionary trend that official diplomats more or less inadvertently cultivate. This section looks at recent articulations of different professional cultures vis-à-vis professional diplomacy, in the context of wider transformations at a global scale, and examines the extent to which old professional 'barriers' to entry in diplomacy are being increasingly breached.

3.1 *Diplomacy as a Distinctive Profession*

The historical process that led to the professionalization of diplomacy, discussed in the previous section, may be also understood in sociological terms. Specifically it can be comprehended as a process of *functional differentiation* of the modern diplomatic system within the wider social system of global modernity, similar to what happened in other domains such as law, accountancy, education or art. In addition to securing its autonomy, this process of differentiation forged during the past two centuries facilitated the configuration of the diplomatic profession as an exclusive domain of sovereign power. The diplomatic profession emerged in parallel to states' hierarchical and centralised control of population and territory, coming under a singular legal international regime, and characterised by social closure and elitism, where exclusion on the basis of gender, class and race were the norm for centuries.

Conceptual opposition between what a diplomat *may* or *may not* be, accompanied by the corresponding social, legal and administrative delimitation, was also crucial for the shaping of the diplomatic profession and as a core element of a world-scale well-differentiated, self-referential diplomatic system. All over the world, diplomacy was a highly regarded profession, and requirements for admission—until the end of the Second World War—frequently included 'proper' social origin and connections, patrimony and even, albeit less frequently, graduation from specific universities. That process allowed for some minor national differences to survive, primarily in terms of formal conditions for recruitment and career development of professional diplomats. A recent survey of peer institutions in 21 countries emphazises the 'diversity in objectives, structures, organization and activities of the institutes' (cfr. Gabrielyan et al. 2016), but basically two traditions may be identified here. In countries such as France, Spain, United Kingdom, United States, Chile and

Japan, diplomats have been a particularly selective group of civil servants, recruited on the basis of competitive examinations and trained by designated ministerial academies or schools. In other cases, like Austria, Denmark, Netherlands, Portugal and Mexico, states have been more open with regard to their training trajectories and diplomats were thus recruited from different professional fields on the basis of merit (cfr. Marques-Guedes 2008).

Convergence also operated through other symbolic mediations related to ceremony and protocol. Diplomatic uniform, for instance, was one of the first civilian uniforms to be established and enforced. First introduced by France in 1781, it was later widely adopted—with only minor variations—by other European states after the 1815 Congress of Vienna, and later by Latin American and Asian countries as well (Hackspiel-Mikosch 2005). Despite initial attempts to defy these conventional understandings of the diplomatic profession, first by the American and French revolutions, and later by the Russian and Chinese revolutions (Armstrong 2008), the diplomatic profession underwent a process of isomorphization. In other words the constitutive elements of the diplomatic profession soon converged across the world, despite huge economic, socio-cultural, political and constitutional differences across established and emergent states (cfr. Bazouni 2001).

Minor differences survived, nonetheless, in terms of internal administrative regulations, organizational culture, working routines and reporting style, within different diplomatic services. Kessler, for instance, compares British and French diplomatic traditions concluding that the former was formally more collegial but rigid in its moral and even religious codes of conduct whilst the latter has been always more competitive and inclined to salient forms of individualism (Kessler 2012: 137). But later she unambiguously concludes that these national specifities have only a minor effect in their actual professional performance (Kessler 2012: 380).

Convergence amongst diverse national models of professional diplomacy, some of them with a long historical trajectory, was thus mediated symbolically through diplomatic law and protocol as well as through diplomatic language. Legal specifications, such as those contained in the 1961 Vienna Convention on Diplomatic Relations, defined what constitutes a diplomatic agent but also how and under what conditions their work is to be performed and their immunities safeguarded (Denza 1997). Diplomatic ceremony and protocol displays a number of delicate rules that only professional diplomats seem entitled to perform (Wood and Serres 1971). Finally, with parallels to other professional languages, such as those cultivated by lawyers and economic auditors, diplomatic language—with its combination of politeness, euphemism and constructive ambiguity—also contributed to underline professional diplomacy as a highly distinctive and stylized practice (Villar 2000; Kurbalija and Slavik 2001; Oglesby 2016). In sum, these symbolic mediations operate what Luhmann called 'systemic closure', thus forging diplomacy as a differentiated field, of which the singular institution of the *diplomatic corps* is perhaps its emblematic symbol (Sofer 2007).

Notwithstanding its historical inertia and pervasiveness, that process of differentiation is nowadays experiencing a sort of regression through *a process of de-differentiation* that began to be visible only a few decades ago. The main reason for this is that the resulting diplomatic system came with its own insufficiencies. The primary functional and normative adjustments that the diplomatic system has adopted in the past decades reveal the limitations of a model that aims to encapsulate socio-economic, cultural, political, environmental and technological complexity within a closed system of relations amongst official representatives of nation-states (cfr. Devin and Toernquist-Chesnier 2012). A critical socio-legal scholar particularly attentive to the transformations of diplomacy has aptly captured the ultimate challenge that these transformations entail:

> What gave diplomatic activity its autonomy was a form of privileged monopoly over a set of highly specialized diplomatic practice and routines. No doubt, the manner in which the symbolic capital was enshrined in these diplomatic practices and routines has been continually challenged and contested by various groups ... however, what is unique in the emergence of the regulatory state and the fragmentations of sovereignty that it implies is the fact that the monopoly of traditional centers with regard to the instruments and activities is being contested. Along with the increasing fragmentation of diplomatic activity is a loss of control over the symbolic capital that gave this privileged monopoly of diplomatic routines.
>
> JAYASURIYA 2005: 54

In the context of a discussion on 'globalization' and diplomacy, Neumann suggested almost a decade ago that official diplomats should reconsider traditional notions of hierarchy, without giving up on it, adopting a 'more proactive' modus operandi when dealing with other social groups or constituencies (Neumann 2008: 27). Traditional forms of diplomatic knowledge, he contends, were dependent on 'specific discursive practices', resulting in a special mode of power relations not reducible to mere strategy nor dominance, that can be consequently called, in accordance with Foucault, a mode of 'governmentality'. The governmentality of modern diplomacy was initially tailored to measure the functional and normative needs of nation-states, permeating the evolving administrative and institutional routines across foreign ministries worldwide. However, it has evolved over time and is now experiencing some adjustments as a result of more active participation from a variety of governmental and non-governmental actors other than official diplomatic representatives. This process demands a more inclusive understanding of diplomatic profession, that is, in the sense of being more receptive to other forms of knowledge and professional skills. The British Foreign and Commonwealth Office (FCO), for instance, seems to be recognizant of this need in a recent report:

> We require deeper expertise in both policy and professional skills, which we should build through longer tours and a human resources system that incentivises individuals to focus on career strengths. We should focus on the new skills required to deliver prosperity and security by 2020 and beyond. We should import the expertise we do not have, and encourage more staff to spend time outside the FCO. We should place greater value on our experts and put them at the heart of policymaking.
>
> FCO 2016: 5

More than the obsolescence of diplomacy these developments thus reveal the never-ending adaptation of diplomacy to the changing historical conditions for its exercise. Slovenian diplomat Milan Jazbec has recently stressed the sociological dimensions of diplomacy. Beyond its elements of continuity, he contends, the concrete 'mode' and 'appearence' of diplomacy, including its professional operationalization, 'depends on and originates from' the specific social and historical situation (Jazbec 2013: 87). In its convincing simplicity, this understanding makes room for a variety of professional interventions other than those deployed by official diplomats, although his analysis is more focused on the new skills and methods needed by official diplomats than on the examination of how other professionals are increasingly engaged in the diplomatic realm in a number of innovative and infuential ways.

As we show in the next section, a plethora of diverse societal actors are increasingly engaged in practices akin to diplomatic ones and are now contributing to what can be called the 'diplomatization' of social life (Neumann 2012). This process of 'diplomatization' is gaining terrain in many different fields, sometimes challenging the primacy of conventional diplomacy as practised by official state representatives, and at other times being easily coopted by official diplomacies. Illustrations of the former abound in domains such as global environmentalism and human rights advocacy, in which non-governmental actors, such as Greenpeace (Bettsil and Corell 2008) and

Amnesty International (Clark 2001) have been crucial in shaping a new international agenda forcing states to react. As for the latter, namely the co-option by official diplomacy of prominent attempts to question its centrality, this is well illustrated by the rapid rise and fall of the so-called non-governmental parallel summits that only a decade ago multiplied all over the world (Gerbaudo and Pianta 2012). However, as Neumann asserts: 'such people are producing knowledge that is often in direct competition with the kind of knowledge that diplomats traditionally attempted to monopolize' (Neumann 2012: 171). Adding a possible explanation for this Neumann notes that:

> Perhaps with the advent of designer capitalism, a form of diplomatization is hitting working life. But if it is, then is exactly because diplomacy's object is indeterminate. A cosmopolitan habitus of the type that has traditionally characterized the diplomat—available, mediating, eager to please—now spread to ever new spheres in post-industrial societies.
>
> NEUMANN 2012: 182

Leonard Seabrooke (2014 and 2015) has consistently examined the conditions in which different forms of professional knowledge—such as those of diplomats, humanitarian activists, army officials or economists—may be constructively combined. In doing so, however, he parts company with those approaches (e.g. Larson 1977; Abbot 1988) that study inter-professional relations in terms of 'established professions competing to control a jurisdiction within a national or transnational context' (Seabrooke 2015: 197). Drawing on White (2008) he focuses instead on how professionals coming from different fields are able to gain positions in political networks that combine different styles and professional knowledge, adapting themselves with flexibility, recognizant of their respective expertise, to the diverse organizational settings and working routines of those other professionals with which they have been invited to engage.

The expansion of the diplomatic agenda due to growing social, economic, environmental and technological interdependence, and the widespread recognition of the need to promote global cooperation through the creation of new regulatory regimes, multilevel institutions for global governance and the multiplication of social demands, defies the conventional understanding of diplomatic profession as mere operational statecraft. However, at the same time, these transformations are also creating unlimited opportunities for the transprofessionalization of diplomacy, understood as a productive development that reflects the expanded space and intensified pace of global interconnections and networks. They also reveal new trends with regard to the partial and selective merging of diplomacy with other engagements on the ground, such as defence and development, in seeking to deliver global governance or engage the 'ungoverned' (Constantinou and Opondo 2016).

This new understanding of diplomacy also goes beyond the widely accepted recognition of the growing importance of a more pro-active diplomatic engagement with foreign publics through public diplomacy (Gregory 2016). It reveals instead that both domestic and foreign publics, in addition to being more or less receptive audiences, are composed of a multiplicity of organized actors, whose representatives are increasingly skilled professionals able to enter in diplomatic intercourse over delicate issues, not only with official diplomatic representatives but also directly with other publics, transgressing the boundaries of officiadom. As Geoffrey Wiseman has recently pointed out with regard to the United States' complicated diplomatic relationships with its adversarial states, along with different forms of governmental engagement with foreign publics, sometimes public diplomacy is 'best left almost entirely to publics dealing directly with other publics' (Wiseman 2015: 299). In other words, according to some observers, the time has come to recognize societal diplomacy as solely able to bolster the transformations needed, although it remains to be defined what such a 'societal diplomacy' should involve (Lagon and Grebowski 2015).

It is important to note, however, that these developments are fostered by wider global transformations that deserve a brief examination as well. Drawing on Bourdieu's conceptual models, Jayasuriya (2004 and 2005) contends that the current situation can be read as the complicated but necessary re-adjustment of diplomacy to the imperatives of a new global political economy. That process affects both the diplomatic system considered as an objective *field*, and the diplomatic *habitus*. The latter is understood as the inter-subjective milieu, slowly formed across historical time, through which diplomats interpret their role and deploy with more or less fortune their professional practices and discourses. The growing gap between the two produces a *hysteresis*, or in other words, a serious mismatch between the *dispositions* of diplomats and their *position* in the new diplomatic realm (Jayasuriya 2005: 53–54). The implications of these are multiple. The effectiveness of official diplomacy is increasingly questioned, and its professionals' performance submitted to new scrutiny. Reduced to the grammars of policy evaluation and auditing, their traditional skills and methods are now considered old-fashioned, unable to deliver tangible results, whilst the validity of such methods for improving their performance remains unclear (cfr. Kleistra and Willigen 2010; Kuus 2016).

With parallels to other professional fields (cfr. Brante 2010), this mismatch produces—along with other changing elements in the wider sociocultural context in which diplomats operate—a destabilization of traditional *regimes of truth* around which the specificity of the diplomatic profession, not only in terms of knowledge and dexterity, but also in terms of sense of belonging and moral codes, was built. However, there are also other important aspects in which this forceful re-adjustment of diplomacy entails some positive implications. Submitted to new public exposure, gender discrimination in diplomacy, for centuries a definitional feature of the diplomatic profession (cfr. Sluga and James 2015), is one aspect in which, despite salient institutional and professional resistance, some important measures have been adopted, and more changes in the near future can be foreseen (cfr. Denechere 2004). The access of women to the diplomatic profession, formally forbidden until quite recently in many countries, is now a common practice across the world, but discrimination remains when high-ranked appointments are examined (cfr. Towns and Niklasson 2016). It can be argued, nonetheless, that a thorough examination of the implications of gender for diplomacy, as indeed with class and race, needs to go beyond what is observable in staff lists ordered by gender and rank. Otherwise, it would be difficult to realize the far-reaching implications of gender-inclusive policies in the transformation of diplomacy. Crucially, gender dimensions are relevant for the internal organization and external performance of diplomatic services, affecting the way in which relevant topics in the global agenda are conceived and approached.

3.2 *Diplomacy as a Paradoxical Profession*

Diplomats occupy a paradoxical position in the contemporary landscape of global professionalism. Whilst the transformation experienced by many other professions can be easily portrayed as a rapid process of transnationalization, with its corresponding implications of de-regulation of services and global marketization, the professional transformations experienced by diplomacy cannot be captured by such a characterisation. To begin with, being as they are a singular body of national civil servants, their profession remains fundamentally attached to the nation-state form. Of course, some exceptions exist, such as civil servants working at multilateral global and regional institutions, with diplomatic status and their corresponding privileges and immunities (cfr. Lemoine 1995), but the diplomatic profession, at least that of official diplomats in the traditional sense (e.g. Harr 1969), remains sheltered from the liberalization of labour markets that has so seriously affected other professional fields (cfr. Faulconbridge and Muzio 2012).

Whilst in many other areas—such as those of legal and business services, security experts, science, education or sports, among others—global liberalization of services radically transformed strongly institutionalized professional systems in just a few decades, transnationalism has affected the diplomatic profession in a significantly different way. After all, it is difficult to find another profession so prominently and transnationally nomadic since ancient times (see Niedner-Kalthoff 2005 and 2006). For that reason, these forces are affecting diplomacy more ostensibly through means other than the simple increase of global mobility.

On the one hand, after decades of mutual rapprochement it is difficult to deny that foreign services all over the world, in their contact with professionals coming from other fields—as with other professional domains (cfr. Hulme 2009; Hedges 2010)—have been able to identify opportunities for mutual learning and fruitful collaboration in many different issues. The shaping of a global environmental protection agenda, for instance, would surely have been impossible without the critical engagement of scientists and ecologists. Although their mobilization was initially received by states with significant reservations (cfr. Auer 1998), their important role was finally recognized, and today they are active players in many regulatory regimes. Indeed collaboration between diplomats and other professionals is frequent at every stage of the negotiation process, and afterwards, when a specific regime or international agreement is implemented. Another important field has been human rights protection and the international fight against criminal impunity. Despite frequent controversies between human rights activists and official diplomatic representatives, institutions like the International Criminal Court would have been very different, and perhaps even impossible, without the valuable contribution of civil society organizations in the early stages of negotiations (Toernquist-Chesnier 2007). This model has been replicated in many other thematic areas.

On the other hand, the proliferation of interventions in the international realm by a variety of influential experts coming from the most disparate fields was initially received, within foreign services across the world, as a form of professional intrusion and irresponsible amateurism. In view of the new activism of NGOs, corporations and think tanks and the irresistible rise of non-career political diplomats, George Kennan (1997) expressed two decades ago his skepticism about the validity of a 'diplomacy without diplomats'. The same year, Richard Langhorne (1997), questioned somewhat rhetorically 'who are the diplomats' and Paul Sharp (1997) more provocatively formulated the critical question: 'Who needs diplomats?'. Reluctance on the side of professional diplomats to accept in their domains professionals from other domains is sometimes well justified, such as in the case of criticisms of political, corporate or celebrity ambassadorial appointees with no credentials other than their proximity to those at the top of national power. However, once the initial disconcert passed, some experienced career diplomats have been able to offer a strong defence of their professions with compelling arguments. Amongst them are two particularly exemplary cases.

Firstly, U.S. careers diplomats, Harry W. Kopp and Charles A. Gillespie (2011), who introduce the profession of diplomacy as follows:

> Among professions it [diplomacy] is an odd one, more like journalism than like law or medicine. It is open to all. Specialized training is available but not required. The skills needed to practice diplomacy at a high level are difficult to master but they are not esoteric. They can be acquired in many fields, including politics, business, the military, and academia. Some of the best practitioners (and also some of the worst) are outsiders who start at the top. Virtually every country that has a department of foreign affairs also has a professional diplomatic service, and almost none but the United States employs amateurs in large numbers [...] A diplomatic service, with ranks gained by merit, also serves to identify the best talents and temperaments as it weeds out the worst.
>
> KOPP AND GILLESPIE 2011: 6–7

Secondly, another experienced career diplomat, former Indian Ambassador, Kishan S. Rana, also expressed his thoughts about the diplomatic profession with great clarity:

> Today, the key roles of embassies are those of promoter, negotiator, communicator, manager, synthesizer, and service provider, across the entire gamut of external affairs. In essence, diplomatic work today is more intensive and proactive than before. This is reflected in the work of bilateral embassies and multilateral missions. The practice of making political appointments of ambassadorships, so widely prevalent in the United States and some other places, undermines the development of professionalism, especially when the appointees do not bring with them public service competence. Although the United States' situation is unique and can be rationalized in its context, in Africa and Latin America such political appointments reduce the efficacy of embassies.
>
> RANA 2013: 11

These views expressed by experienced diplomats are illustrative of what classical sociology of professions considered a collective mobilization project understood as a process of regulatory capture (cfr. Freidon 1982). This is a process that Larson summarized as follows:

> I see professionalization as the process by which producers of special services sought to constitute and control a market for their expertise. Because marketable expertise is a crucial element in the structure of modern inequality, professionalization appears also as a collective assertion of special social status and as a collective process of upward social mobility.
>
> LARSON 1977: XVI

This view tends to concentrate on the 'intricate negotiations between the professions and other actors such as the state that lead to the maintenance and reproduction of professional practices, privileges and values' as Faulconbridge and Muzio (2012: 137) aptly summarize. However, that vision of professional mobilization as a project of market control seems inadequate in those cases, like diplomacy, in which the central role of the state is indisputable, as compared to other cases that seem to be more clearly driven by market forces (Dingwall 1999). For the first case at least, it can be argued that if the state played a critical role in the moment of the creation of a profession around a set of services and skills—as it happened with diplomacy—it will play an equally important role in its possible deprofessionalization, or what we prefer to call transprofessionalization, emphazising instead the positive potential that these transformations entail. Interestingly, this is something that experienced career diplomats, as illustrated by those quoted above, seem to be well aware of, even if they apparently still seem to be attached to an understanding of diplomacy as a national and public service not submitted to any critical transnational or privatizing force.

This is another feature of the current transformations in the diplomatic profession in which the results are rather paradoxical. Whilst in other professions 'many of the most powerful actors involved in the institutionalization of professional privileges and practices increasingly seek to develop professional regulations, norms and cultures outside the confines of Westphalian state regimes through forms of transnational professional projects tied to the imperatives of neoliberal capitalism' (Faulconbridge and Muzio 2012: 139), diplomats remain attached to a notion of public service; an attachment which is increasingly rare amongst lawyers, business consultants, sports professionals or scientists. However, in view of the global diffusion of power and the rise of the regulatory state, it is arguable that if the logic of global markets stimulates the rise of global professions, sooner or later it will also foster the emergence of *global* professional diplomats. Yet, the question should not be viewed as a simple dissolution of the public and national domains, but rather as an expression of a complex and contentious process of readjusting positions between 'public' and 'private' power, as well as 'national' and 'transnational' power, in a new global order that acquires diverse configurations in various contexts. Hocking aptly portrays this when he notes that:

> In some contexts, nongovernmental organizations (NGOs) are portrayed as opponents of government, disrupting World Trade Organization summits and, for example, helping to defeat the attempt to frame a Multilateral Agreement on Investment. On the other hand, governments rely extensively on NGOs in humanitarian assistance and for the delivery of foreign aid programmes. Without NGOs, the agreement to outlaw the use of landmines, would, in all probability, not have seen the light of day. On another plane, firms are assuming a central role in key areas of trade policy and in developing global strategies in the battle against HIV-AIDS.
>
> HOCKING 2004: 147

As Fourcade indicates, however, for 'professionals whose work remains bounded by national regulations the opening of borders may signify a quite dramatic jurisdictional change' (Fourcade 2006: 148). An illustration of this is the launching of the European External Action Service (EEAS). Initially received with caution by member states' foreign services it was later approached with curiosity and then embraced by both senior and junior career professionals, who saw it as opportunity to progress. But this was perhaps also facilitated because, despite its interstitial character and singular combination of national and supranational elements and the diversity of recruitment and training modes, the EEAS' public character and vocation is not in dispute (cfr. Carta 2012; Adler-Nissen 2013; Batora 2013; Berger 2013). As for the case of global private diplomats, a possible model would be that provided by prominent international legal firms and business consultants that offer their expertise across the world (Dezalay 2004; Fourcade 2006), and which are also emerging in the diplomatic field. These include prestigious, albeit non-profit, advisory groups like Independent Diplomat (Ross 2007) and for-profit global consultancies like The Ambassador Partnership.

According to Stephen Gill (2012), however, many of these practices can be seen as the adaptation of diplomacy to the 'common sense' of global liberalism; an extension of the managerial transformation that has been led by legal consultants, policy advisors, accountants and experts, to which even development and humanitarian volunteers would be unable to escape (Lacey and Ilcan 2006; cfr. Constantinou and Opondo 2016). These new *unofficial* diplomats, even more than the *official* ones, can thus be seen as the real 'operators of globalization' in the sense advanced by Kauppi and Madsen:

> Going behind the facade of global institutions and instead focusing on the arguably deeper structures of global governance, we can also start to explain the emergence of new forms of power as they develop around new transnational power elites operating in, around, and beyond a growing number of international institutions.
>
> KAUPPI AND MADSEN 2014: 324

But the activities of many other 'operators of globalization' can also be read as forms of genuine contestation and critical political agency, not so easily reducible to co-option. Reflecting on this, Bertrand Badie (2008) recognizes in some of these intrusions a new and vibrant democratizing force of diplomacy, yet one that the diplomatic establishment is generally able either to co-opt or to deactivate. However, Badie also recommends considering the wider implications of engaging diplomatically with these new actors. To the extent to which they are sometimes expressive of serious social grievances and divides, he contends, they are elusive to 'forced conversions' and may also serve to prepare new forms of political conflict (Badie 2008: 276).

Many other professional fields, such as social work, elite sport, nursing, informatics, or education and cab-driving, have experienced significant changes that come to destabilize an otherwise straightforward professional identity. In these fields, old divisions have also been transgressed, and experienced professionals are now subject to new and unexpected pressures relating not only to their credentials and skills, but also their power, status, gender, race, knowledge, organization, methods, accountability, regulation and so on, making them feel insecure and under constant supervision in performing their profession (cfr. Dent and Whitehead 2002). Similarly, diplomats are not the sole professionals that at some moment became alarmed by legal and political processes of deprofessionalization that apparently put the credibility and sustainability of their professional field at risk (cfr. Henrikson 1999). Social workers and care-givers, for instance, have suffered acutely from the privatization and marketization of social and health policies in many OECD countries, and only recently have they, in some cases, been able to recover terrain (cfr. Duyvendak 2005). By contrast British diplomat, and former Ambassador to Lebanon, Tom Fletcher, seeks to redress the crisis of official diplomacy through more drastic measures. He contends that diplomacy is too important to be left to diplomats and proclaims that the new ideal diplomat will be a 'lobbyst, leader, communicator, pioneer, entrepreneur, activist, campaigner, advocate' but will not be a career diplomat (Fletcher 2016: 208) More frequently, however, as various reports produced by official diplomatic services all over the world illustrate, traditional diplomats tend to combine the proud self-assertion of their professional distinctiveness with the reflective recognition of its necessary adaptation to a new reality:

> Diplomacy is a profession, and should be defined as such. Its key tasks are connection, negotiation and representation. The corresponding values and expertise must also be defined to take account of the demands of the hybrid world... knowledge of foreign countries, forums and local networks, and the negotiating and other skills required to find one's way around them, are in any case key to the further definition of the profession. Today's hybrid world calls for diplomats who can switch back and forth between different worlds—who, as it were, have the chameleon-like ability to adapt to different networks. Other essential skills that they require in order to operate in networks are enterprise and an open outlook.
>
> MODERNISING DUTCH DIPLOMACY 2013: 21

Perhaps the best way to understand the multiple transformations that diplomacy is experiencing nowadays is to accept, as suggested by Evetts (2010: 790), the contested nature of the meaning of professionalism itself. What is certain is that these transformations are not the result of a single, great design, but the outcome of multiple forms of individual, albeit socially and institutionally embedded, relational agency (cfr. Harrington 2015). This will be explored in more detail in the following section.

4 Phenomenology: Diplomacy Transprofessionalized

Thus far in this paper we have sought to trace the origins of diplomacy as a profession and to sketch out how official state diplomacy has morphed, adapted and been reconfigured in the face of increasingly global demands of market forces and transnationalism. Our aim in this final substantive section is to further complicate the idea of a multi-dimensional diplomatic landscape by turning our attention beyond the political unit of the state. Not only has there been sustained engagement with diplomatic practices by representatives of government agencies well beyond foreign ministries, but representatives of non-state actors have also had an increasingly professionalized presence on the diplomatic stage.

4.1 *The Proliferation of 'New' Diplomatic Actors and Their 'Professionals'*

There is growing consensus amongst scholars and practitioners that diplomacy in the late 20th and early 21st centuries is changing, and changing fast. Explanations for such dynamism often centre on shifts in the balance of geopolitical power since the end of the Cold War, the myriad effects of both accelerating globalization and a rise in regionalism on diplomatic practice, and rapid technological and communication advances leading to the emergence of digital diplomacy (Bjola and Holmes 2015; Kerr and Wiseman 2013). Underpinning many of these narratives of change is the observation that there has been a proliferation of 'new' actors in the diplomatic field working in parallel to, in partnership with or in competition with state diplomats. This 'polylateral' form of diplomacy (Wiseman 2004) includes supranational and subnational diplomatic services, and the engagement of international NGOs, unrecognised states, multinational corporations, and even influential individuals in different modes of diplomacy.

The debunking of the traditional assumption that diplomacy is the special preserve of the state is, of course, nothing new. Since the late 1970s scholars of the English School of IR have posited that diplomacy is a central institution of the 'international society' of states (Bull 1977; Watson 1984; Sharp and Wiseman 2007). More recently, the emergence of critical diplomatic theory has seen attention turn to the role of diplomatic cultures (Dittmer and McConnell 2016), 'sustainable diplomacy' (Constantinou and Der Derian 2010) and intergroup dynamics (Sharp 2009). Attending specifically to the multiplication of non-state actors on the diplomatic stage has been a growing body of work loosely labelled 'new diplomacy' (Cooper et al 2002; Riordan 2003). The likes of NGOs (Betsill and Corell 2008), indigenous communities (Beier 2010), supranational organisations (e.g. the European External Action Service, Balfour et al. 2015; Kuus 2014; Carta 2012), cities (Acuto 2013), overseas territories (Adler-Nissen and Gad 2013), sub-state governments (Aldecoa and Keating 1999; Cornago 2010), celebrities (Cooper 2007) and religious leaders (Megoran 2010) are analysed in this scholarship as distinctive new actors in world politics.

This is a rich and diverse body of scholarship, but one which has not escaped critique. The proliferating set of prefixes—paradiplomacy, NGO diplomacy, business diplomacy, celebrity diplomacy etc.—can be viewed as offering an analytically limited 'explanation by naming' (Sending et al. 2011: 529). In response, Ole Jacob Sending and colleagues propose a productive line of enquiry focused around the '*relational* nature of contemporary changes in the diplomatic practice' (Ibid., emphasis in the original), attending not to the relative significance of state versus non-state actors but to how the institution and practice of diplomacy is being reconfigured by the evolving engagement of a wide range of players. The presentism of 'new diplomacy' has also been challenged, with persuasive arguments being made that religious figures, indigenous communities, cities and regions have long sought to cultivate foreign relations through engaging in formal diplomatic practices and are thus by no means 'new' diplomatic actors (Hamilton and Langhorne 1995; Bátora and Hynek 2014; Beier 2010). Noé Cornago (2013 and 2016) pushes this argument further and asserts that expressions of pluralism in the diplomatic realm that are today lauded as novel were in fact crucial in the formative processes of modern diplomacy itself.

Cognizant of such arguments, we aim to build on scholarship which has used the multiplication of diplomatic actors to ask productive questions of the nature of diplomacy itself. These include: the extent to which the role of non-state actors is changing, challenging or extending the nature and quality of diplomacy; which aspects of diplomatic work these actors emulate; how diplomatic practice in turn conditions these actors' strategies; and the broader questions of who is, and who should be, a legitimate actor in international relations, and what these developments tell us about changes in the international system (see Beier 2007: 10; Cooper and Hocking 2000; Cornago 2013; McConnell et al. 2012; Sending et al. 2015: 10)?

In what remains of this paper, we seek to offer insights into these questions through the lens of 'transprofessionalization'. We first turn attention to the 'new' skills and knowledges that non-state actors bring to the diplomatic realm, from expertise and specialised knowledge pertinent to the increasing prevalence of issue-based diplomacy to innovations in digital technology and advocacy strategies. We then examine how non-state diplomats seek to 'learn the game' of diplomacy, tracing out the strategies of mimicry and socialization whereby these actors emulate formal diplomatic practices, and exploring how non-state actors use diplomatic tropes to fashion new geopolitical possibilities. Cross-cutting these empirical concerns is an effort to draw on a broader range of literatures in order to analyse the changing landscape of 'professional' diplomacy than is currently the case. As such, we turn attention to concepts and framings from scholarship on the role and power of non-state actors in international politics (e.g. Keck and Sikkink 1998; Haas 1992; Finnemore and Sikkink 1998; Bob 2005), sociological analyses (e.g. Gheciu 2005) and theories from cultural anthropology (Victor Turner's work on liminality) and postcolonial studies (e.g. Homi Bhabha's notions of mimicry and hybridity).

4.2 *Promoting 'New' Diplomatic Skills: Functional Specificity and Creative Experimentation*

Given the diverse range of political actors now engaged with diplomatic practice it is perhaps not surprising that they bring a vast array of new skills, knowledge and professional assemblages to the field. What *is* surprising is the lack of critical analysis of the effects that these distinctive modes of expertise are having on established diplomatic practices and institutions. One possible explanation for this oversight is that, to date, there has been a remarkable lack of sustained and productive dialogue between literature on new diplomacy and the now sizeable body of scholarship on the role and power of non-state actors in the international arena (Sending et al 2011: 533). The latter ranges from pioneering work on transnational advocacy networks (Keck and Sikkink 1998) and epistemic communities (Haas 1992), to analysis of international norm dynamics (Finnemore and Sikkink 1998) and global civil society networks (Bob 2005; Castells 2008). Here, we seek to trace points of connection between these framings and the emerging dynamics of non-state involvement in international diplomacy.

Trying to distil what typifies the nature of non-state actors' engagement in diplomacy is a challenging task. One place to start is to consider the preparedness for international negotiation and representation of those outside of the formal diplomatic corps. In essence, without the strictures of formal diplomatic training, or having to subscribe to a particular national tradition and culture of diplomacy, non-state actors are freer to experiment with different practices. As such, the modes of diplomacy adopted are often characterised by significant levels of trial and error. Michael Keating has traced this phenomenon in the context of paradiplomacy where he has noted that 'regions experiment to see what works and what is cost-effective' (1999: 13) with their diplomatic strategies being shaped by both their motivations—whether economic, cultural or political—and the opportunity structures that they face. This, he argues, leads to diplomacy which is 'more functionally specific and targeted, often opportunistic experimental' (Keating 1999: 11). Whilst acknowledging that different types of actor bring different sets of skills, experiences and knowledge to their diplomatic roles, common trends around functional specificity and creative experimentation can be traced. We explore each of these in turn.

Diplomacy is, of course, only one of many strategies and fields of engagement for non-state actors. Unlike foreign ministries, diplomatic practice is not their primary raison d'être. They therefore seek to engage with the diplomatic realm with specific end goals in mind, whether that is addressing loopholes in international human rights law, protecting the language rights for a minority community, securing stewardship of particular natural resources, lobbying for the creation of new environmental protection treaties or banning the use of specific weapons. The implication of this functionally specific engagement with diplomacy is that the areas that non-state actors bring to the international diplomatic arena are those where they have particular expertise. And it is precisely this expertise—and the specialised knowledge and information that underpin it—that is a key source of power for non-state actors in international relations (Keck and Sikkink 1998; Haas 1992).

The nature of this expertise varies greatly. It may be scientific knowledge of particular environmental processes or practices such as climate change, biodiversity loss or whaling, testimonial evidence of human rights abuses collated by an NGO, or on-the-ground knowledge that an indigenous community or opposition movement has about land grabs or disputed elections. Given that issues of concern—and indeed international crises—around the environment, human rights and political conflict are invariably highly complex, riddled with technical uncertainties and cannot be addressed solely by states, such scientific or first-hand knowledge is deemed essential for 'understanding the nature of the problems and the implications of various policy alternatives under consideration' (Corell and Betsill 2008: 23). NGOs in particular are playing an increasingly important role in epistemic communities, networks of knowledge-based experts who have 'an authoritative claim to policy-relevant knowledge' (Haas 1992: 3). Indeed their information gathering capabilities and generation of novel policy ideas are proving to be instrumental in 'helping states identify their interests, framing the issues for collective debate, proposing specific policies, and identifying salient points for negotiation' (Haas 1992: 2; Cooper and Hocking 2000). As such, the knowledge of these non-state experts is often perceived as a valuable resource by established state diplomats and the ability to provide such information is a key mechanism by which these actors gain credibility, legitimacy and—to varying degrees—influence on the international stage.

It is not just expert knowledge that NGOs, indigenous communities, political dissidents and the like can bring to the diplomatic table. What augments their influence, even when they are barred from accessing the primary forums of international diplomacy, is the combining of expertise with popular pressure, whether in the form of petitions, street protests, boycotts or direct action. Well-resourced and long established campaigning NGOs are perhaps the most successful at this, combining knowledge from on the ground monitoring and witnessing techniques with worldwide publicity campaigns and moral pressure to appeal to governments and international organisations to improve the likes of environmental and human rights practices. However, it is far from the case that all political campaigns and movements become the focus of high profile lobbying. As Clifford Bob (2005) documents, the choice of which issues influential transnational NGOs such as Greenpeace, Friends of the Earth, and Amnesty International decide to promote is often a political rather than moral one. Echoing this, Charli Carpenter notes that 'while a number of significant campaigns since the early 1990s have resulted in bans of particular weapons, at least as many equivalent systems have gone unscrutinized and uncondemned by transnational campaigners' (2011: 69) and calls for more sustained analytical attention to be paid to the process of organizational issue selection *within* NGOs.

For those campaigns that do receive attention from leading NGOs, international negotiations form only one part of a far broader web of advocacy activities across a scalar range of political arena, from the decision making of individuals to national level policy making and the promotion of global civil society (Betsill and Corell 2008). As scholars have documented, such strategies have had notable successes, from Amnesty International's significant impact on the establishment of international standards on human rights (Clark 2001), to the success of the International Campaign to Ban Landmines in bringing about the Mine Ban Treaty (Ottawa Treaty, 1997), Greenpeace's campaign to establish an Antarctic-Environmental Protocol, and the Inuit Circumpolar Council's negotiations on resource stewardship and cultural self-determination (Shadian 2016). The role of such non-state actors in international negotiations thus has the effect of broadening the types of knowledge, information and strategies within the formal diplomatic realm. It also reflects the increasing professionalization of non-state actors where there has been a shift over recent decades from a reliance on untrained volunteers to a growing cadre of experienced NGO negotiators, indigenous expert elites and private diplomats. The resultant enhancement of non-state diplomats' skills in terms of representation, communication and negotiation is reflected precisely in the ability of NGOs to 'breed new ideas; advocate, protest, and mobilize public support; [and] do legal, scientific, technical, and policy analysis' (Mathews 1997: 55 cited in Cooper and Hocking 2000: 368). As Cooper and Hocking note, this is seen in contrast to claims that, in light of bureaucratic downsizing across many governments due to financial constraints, the state has 'fallen behind in terms of core skills such as information gathering, the evaluation and nurturing of ideas, and communication' (2000: 368).

One area where the disparity between state and non-state skills is particularly apparent is that of digital technology. As a number of scholars have documented, the recent proliferation of digital initiatives in diplomatic corps and foreign ministries constitutes a revolution in the practice of diplomacy (Bjola and Holmes 2015; Dizard 2001). Yet foreign ministries have, in many cases, been both slow to realise the potential of digital technology to transform how international relations are handled, and wary about adapting to the rapidly evolving communication technology landscape. In contrast, with their reliance on close coordination and their significantly lower operating costs, new digital technologies favour organisations based on decentralised networks, unlike the traditional hierarchies of foreign ministries. In turn, the 'flexible and agile structure of NGOs [and other non-state actors] allows them to adapt well to the use of new technology' (Cooper and Hocking 2000: 368) and they are subsequently often more familiar with, and are more creative and effective in their use of, social media. Thus, in contrast to foreign ministries, non-state actors have, in many cases, already embraced the social media age and are institutionally adapted to the digital landscape. As a result, they have the potential to lead by example in the realm of 'new' diplomacy.[1]

More generally it can be argued that the innovation of non-state actors in advocacy strategies, modes of communication and transnational networking brings to the fore possibilities for generating spaces for creative thinking within diplomacy. Freed of the constraints of adhering to particular national agendas and engaging in international diplomacy without the formal accoutrements—or indeed regulations or media scrutiny—that accompany the official diplomatic corps, non-state actors are in a position where they are able to try out different modes of diplomatic practice. This has the potential to place them in a privileged role in comparison to state diplomats as, free from the obligations of full-membership of the international system, they are able to be more flexible in who they seek to engage with and how. As a result they are able to direct their (generally limited) resources towards maximising their direct interests (Dickson 2014). In the case of sub-state regions, this has included the Finnish region of Åland using its 'lived history' and special status as an autonomous region to practice norm entrepreneurship (Finnemore and Sikkink 1998) in the form of advocating for the 'Åland example' as a model for international conflict resolution (Wigell 2013). In a different context the Bavarian government has adeptly used its relatively compact scale and commercial 'approachability' to foster productive diplomatic connections with international investors and trade partners (Dickson 2014). Crucially, such capitalising on intrinsic qualities that a sub-state actor possesses is undertaken whilst simultaneously being able to

---

1 Given the potential for non-state actors to lead the way in digital diplomacy the paucity of research in this field is surprising. To date the focus of scholarly and practitioner publications on digital diplomacy has been on state diplomats and foreign ministries (for an exception see Corrie (2015) on the International Criminal Court's use of digital technology).

deliberately avoid controversial diplomatic issues which the national level government is involved with, by emphasising both their distinctiveness and their subordinate status. This leads therefore to an experimentation in diplomatic practices which, in turn, has the potential effect of making diplomacy itself more collaborative, flexible and open.

Particular characteristics of different non-state actors are key to enabling this flexibility and innovation in diplomacy. In the case of NGOs, transnational corporations and de facto religious communities their ability to 'represent constituencies that are not bounded by territory but by common values, knowledge, and/or interests related to a specific issue' (Betsill and Corell 2008: 2) means that their diplomatic practice is essentially deterritorialised. Therefore, in contrast to state diplomats, these actors can more easily and effectively represent issues that transcend inter-state boundaries, and can claim to represent globe-spanning constituencies based on gender, ethnicity and particular value systems or, in the case of rights based advocacy, humankind itself. In thus being able to claim a virtual and symbolic rather than territorially bounded form of authority (Sending et al. 2015), such actors are starting to shift the mode of representation within international diplomacy. Yet for other non-state actors, the opposite trend can be observed: for indigenous communities and many stateless nations territory is of *heightened* importance to their articulation of diplomacy. Indeed as Marshall Beier (2010) argues, it is precisely the strong connections to land that underpins indigeneity, and the tension between such connections and the sovereignty claims of territorial states, that means that these communities' advocacy activities should be seen as indigenous *diplomacies* rather than indigenous social movements.

Another characteristic that a number of non-state actors share is a propensity for large-scale coalition building and the pooling of information and expertise. We can think here of the Inuit Circumpolar Council, well-established partnerships among subnational governments, such as the Council of Local Authorities and Regions of Europe, or transnational advocacy networks which Keck and Sikkink define as alliances of 'actors working internationally on an issue, who are bound together by shared values, a common discourse and dense exchanges of information and services' (1998: 2). Such networks have been particularly effective in achieving policy changes in issue-based diplomacy—for example around women's rights, labour rights and regulation of the arms trade—where they have made effective use of institutionally attuned cognitive frames to encourage policy action and shifts in international norms. In these cases the network itself enhances the influence of individual actors by 'amplifying their voice and promoting greater efficiency in gathering and disseminating information' (Corell and Betsill 2008: 39). However, in other cases, it is the flexibility and dynamism of non-state actors themselves that promotes their diplomatic effectiveness. As Constantinou notes, unlike conventional government diplomats, 'new diplomatic actors can emerge overnight, creating new diplomatic spaces and channels of communication, if strong commitment over an issue exists, acquiring symbolic power that can exceed that of states and shape events in dramatic fashion, positively or negatively' (2013: 158).

Underpinning this organisational flexibility, and the creative experimentation in diplomacy that it enables, is the often ambiguous status of many of these actors. Existing 'betwixt and between' (Turner 1969: 95) the categories of state and non-state are the likes of aspiring states (whether stateless nations, exile governments or de facto states), sub-state actors (in the form of paradiplomacy) and 'fringe players' such as the Holy See and the Sovereign Military Order of Malta (see Bátora and Hynek 2014). In each of these cases of 'geopolitical liminality' (McConnell forthcoming) the actors involved are positioned both inside and outside the international system. They are usually excluded from the modern diplomatic order, but have nevertheless sought to carve out subject positions, repertoires of practice and alternative spaces of formal diplomacy. Crucially, therefore, these actors are not political 'others' to conventional diplomacy, but at the same time they are also experimenting with and adapting culturally specific modes of statecraft. This liminal and often hybrid status thus enables non-state actors to do *particular* 'things' in their diplomacy. For example, the ambiguous status of regional diplomats offers them considerable scope to operate in various networks either simultaneously or sequentially. As Francesca Dickson (2014) notes, sub-state governments have the potential to 'free ride' on the foreign policy of their national state. They can emphasise their distinctiveness when this has positive connotations (e.g. the Scottish Government's anti-nuclear stance), but when a distinct international profile is not desirable or beneficial then they can revert to deferring to their host state's diplomatic status. Meanwhile the Holy See strategically uses its status ambiguity to 'present different symbolic orientation within the Westphalian diplomatic system' (Bátora and Hynek 2014: 80). This includes its articulation of both sacred and secular diplomacy and the fact that its 'ambassadors' (nuncios) are both strangers in the host nation but also an integral part of the Catholic community of that host (Chong and Troy 2011).

Ambiguous actorness also facilitates the maintenance of a particular international profile whereby representatives of non-state actors can *choose* as and when to don a diplomatic 'hat'. This is especially apparent in the case of unrecognised states, nations and peoples where many of the individuals representing these polities were, in previous 'careers', resistance fighters, pro-independence rebels or human rights activists before they sought to engage in international diplomacy. Such career biographies thus raise the question of where the boundary lies between a 'diplomat'—a bona fide representative and a professional negotiator—and an 'activist'—someone advocating change through campaigning. In light of these threshold subject positions, McConnell (forthcoming) suggests the notion of *geopolitical shapeshifters*: actors that look different at different times and in different settings. Neither 'self' (state) nor 'other' (non-state), they occupy an in-between position, but this is not a static or fixed status. This is a dynamism that can, in many cases, be productive. Its embracing of inbetweenness with regards to political status opens up diplomatic opportunities that are closed to those who have been assigned more fixed political categories. Self-identified political activists rarely gain entry into the forums of international diplomacy and formal state diplomats run into trouble when they become 'too activist' as the case of the former British Ambassador to Uzbekistan Craig Murray attests (Murray 2006).

Whilst liminal subject positions can, in certain circumstances, be harnessed for strategic advantage, the gaps between bodies of professional knowledge can also be exploited by non-state actors. An intriguing example of this are economic consultancies which undertake a brokering role between states and unrecognised polities and communities. Leonard Seabrooke makes a persuasive argument that these actors—such as STATT consulting and Independent Diplomat—engage in 'epistemic arbitrage' whereby they 'mediate between knowledge pools for strategic advantage and... become the "arbiters" on what knowledge and practices are most influential in their area of transnational governance' (2014: 49). Such practices may be dismissed as opportunistic, but they crucially expose the taken for granted norms of diplomatic work and representation, and unsettle distinctions between 'what is diplomatic activity and what is not, and who, therefore, are diplomats and who are not' (Hamilton and Langhorne 1995: 3).

4.3 *Mimicking 'Old' Diplomatic Skills: Socialization and Creative Subversion*

Underpinning this understanding of non-state diplomatic actors as liminal, hybrid and occupying an ambiguous position vis-à-vis 'official' state diplomacy is the assumption that their diplomacy looks and sounds similar to that of states. Take, for example, the Tibetan Government-in-Exile, an unrecognised administration formerly headed by the Dalai Lama and which is based in Dharamsala in northwest India. Given its lack of legal status, it is logical to expect that this polity engages solely with aspects of public and cultural diplomacy. And to a significant extent this is the case with Tibetan diplomacy drawing heavily on the 'national brand' of the Dalai Lama, Tibetan Buddhism and romanticized images of Shangri-la (Anand 2007). But, the exile government also seeks to create an 'international persona' through emulating traditional, state-based diplomatic practices. It has established a Department of Information and International Relations which assumes the conventional roles of a foreign ministry including a protocol office, it arranges for exchange visits for exile Tibetan MPs and their counterparts in Western democracies, and it runs a series of unofficial embassies in eleven cities across the world which provide consular services, maintain direct contacts with parliamentarians and foreign ministries and coordinate the Dalai Lama's official visits (McConnell 2016).

Whilst not mirroring state structures per se, NGOs also emulate the functions of state delegates in that 'they represent the interests of their constituencies, they engage in information exchange, they negotiate, and they provide policy advice' (Betsill 2008: 205). Moreover, as Bátora and Hynek note, this resemblance to traditional interstate diplomacy can often be advantageous:

> Adaptation, strategic realignment and institutional mimicry all allow fringe players to look similar to states proper. Yet . . . they further cultivate their distinctness and maintain traditions . . . their fringe position in the international system allows such actors to be more flexible and innovative as they can also draw on and utilize structures, environments and/or practices from different institutional orders.
>
> BATORA AND HYNEK 2014: 77

As discussed above, this ability to engage with different institutional orders simultaneously is an important characteristic of sub-state diplomacy, and indeed the notion of resembling state diplomacy is implied in the very term paradiplomacy which suggests a 'second-order set of activities, pale imitation of "real" diplomacy' (Hocking 1999: 21). Yet to dismiss regional diplomacy—and non-state diplomacy more generally—as of 'second order' to state diplomacy is to unhelpfully downplay the agency of such actors. The question then arises as to how to understand non-state diplomats' engagements with the 'old' or traditional skills of diplomacy?

One potentially productive framing is that of mimicry (McConnell et al. 2012). With its roots in literary theory and postcolonial studies, the notion of mimicry as formulated by Homi Bhabha refers to the subversive adoption of a culture, an adoption that is always incomplete. Bhabha defines mimicry as 'the desire for a reformed, recognizable Other, as a subject of a difference that is almost the same, but not quite,' (1984: 126, emphasis in original) and, whilst he refers specifically to the identity practices of empire, the notion can be usefully transposed to the realm of diplomacy. As McConnell et al argue, mimicry 'demonstrates how non state diplomacies draw on, mimic and intervene in the realm of formal political action in ways which both promote "official" state diplomacy as an ideal and dilute its distinction from other, "unofficial" diplomacies' (2012: 804). Through the lens of mimicry, therefore, non-state diplomacy can be seen to both reproduce and reinforce traditional interstate diplomacy and the authority of states more generally by emulating modes of state diplomacy, and also subvert that legitimacy by reducing the gap between the 'real' and the 'mimic' through the appropriation of diplomatic practices for their own purposes.

With regards to the context of diplomatic skills and practices, the framing of mimicry opens up two questions: *how* do non-state diplomats learn and mimic the 'old' skills of state-based diplomacy; and *why* do they invest time and resources into this mimicry? In terms of where non-official diplomats turn to in order to learn the 'trade' of diplomacy, the picture that emerges is revealing of diplomatic practice more generally. As Kissinger (1995) acknowledges, diplomacy is both an art and a science: there may be a professional canon for diplomats, but essentially 'it rests on a huge stock of practical knowledge that cannot be learned from books' (Pouliot and Cornut 2015: 307). Learning through experience and on the job training is certainly key for non-state diplomats but there are also more formal modes of training and mentorship. Some of this is provided by national diplomatic training academies, or by NGOs such as Minority Rights Group, and advice and mentorship is also offered by organisations like Independent Diplomat, a non-profit consultancy which provides diplomatic services to unrecognised governments.

Central to such training is the socialization of non-state diplomats in the norms of international diplomacy. This has striking parallels to sociological institutionalist literature in International Relations which looks at the spread of rational bureaucratic norms through the diffusion of similar institutional forms across different contexts, for example, Alexandra Gheciu's (2005) research on how NATO 'taught' new member states—Czech Republic and Romania—new norms. Just as nascent states are inducted into the rules of the society or family of states, so representatives of non-state organisations and polities are socialised in the norms and practices that underpin interstate diplomacy as it currently stands, including tacit knowledge regarding how to 'guard secrets, mediate and call on precedents from law and how to manoeuvre with national foreign ministries, NGOs and international organisations' (Seabrooke 2015: 204).

One interesting agent of socialization is the Unrepresented Nations and Peoples Organization (UNPO), a membership organisation of almost 50 indigenous, minority and occupied peoples which, due to their lack of legal recognition, are formally excluded from the conventional fora of international politics. Central to the UNPO's remit is the provision of training on how 'diplomats' of member communities can best present themselves and their cause to the international community in ways that garners not only sympathy but also political and material support. Through UNPO run training events (with both 'in house' trainers and expertise brought in from human rights and lobbying NGOs) representatives of member communities are taught to package up their national cause in a form digestible to the discourses of international diplomacy. Essentially this involves translating their community's grievances, experiences of oppression and human rights abuses and claims to independence in ways which strip away the emotion and passionate nationalism, instead framing it in the discourses of international law. These non-state elites thus both draw on cultural values from the communities they represent and adopt and re-work ostensibly Western discourses of democracy, human rights and environmentalism.

But of course adaptation to the norms of international diplomacy is performative as well as discursive. Echoing Merje Kuus' (2014) work on newly recruited diplomats of the EEAS, unofficial diplomats also need to learn the comportment, the practices and the mores of state-based diplomacy (Bourdieu 1977). Here the UNPO plays a role in 'professionalizing' community leaders/activists into diplomats through training them in the performances of diplomacy. As well as briefings and workshops this training is also delivered through simulation and role play exercises of specific UN Committees and through the Organization's General Assembly. The latter events are opportunities to practice and rehearse diplomatic protocol. With this emulation of the UN system these General Assemblies are rehearsal spaces: they are sites where UNPO members can try out being diplomats, become familiar with the spaces of national parliaments and practice lobbying skills.

Turning to the question of *why* non-state actors, to varying degrees, mimic formal state diplomacy, the reasons centre on a range of political goals, from seeking legitimacy in the international sphere to fashioning new geopolitical possibilities. In the case of polities which aspire to statehood such as de facto states, governments in exile and stateless nations, such investment of time, energy and resources in emulating the symbols of formal diplomacy is made because these actors see such conventional practices and tropes of diplomacy as central to attempting to play the state game, being heard on the international stage and constructing political legitimacy (McConnell et al 2012; Wilson and McConnell 2015). As noted above, examples such as Somaliland, the Turkish Republic of Northern Cyprus and Nagorno Karabakh mimic a wide range of key practices and discourses and institutions of official state diplomacy in its traditional guise including the establishment of unofficial embassies, adherence to diplomatic protocols, formation of multilateral organizations and convening of general assemblies and summits. These institutions and practices are perceived as key leverages of power, demonstrating an 'environmental fit within the Westphalian system' (Bátora and Hynek 2014: 83) and credibility to what is often deemed clandestine and threatening.

However it is not only for the claiming of political legitimacy that key practices, materialities and discourses of orthodox diplomacy are imitated. Such mimicry can also constitute a mode of political protest. An iconic example of this is the Aboriginal Tent Embassy, established on 'Australia Day' in 1972 when four young men claimed to establish an embassy by plating a beach umbrella on the lawn in front of Parliament House, Canberra (Foley et al. 2013). The Embassy quickly became a symbol of aboriginal struggle for rights and justice and was one of the most significant indigenous political demonstrations of the twentieth century. While formally citizens of Australia since 1967, the ambassadors claimed that, since Aboriginal people were effectively aliens in their own land, they needed an embassy to represent their interests to the Australian state just like any other group of foreign nationals. Indeed, in naming their protest site an *Embassy* the activists effectively 'turned one of the foremost symbolic spaces of the colonial state against itself' (Iveson 2013: 253), and drew attention to the living conditions of many Aboriginals in Australia. As such, the 'pointedly antimonumental architecture' of the embassy—which, over the years, consisted of a collection of tents, a shipping container and traditional shelters—demonstrates 'both the dispossession from and continued possession of Aboriginal land' (Muldoon and Schaap 2012: 540). At first glance, therefore, the Embassy can be seen to mimic and parody the sovereign state, with its flying of the Australian Aboriginal Flag, appointment of a minister for Caucasian affairs and claim of the right to negotiate with the Australian state. However, as Muldoon and Schaap argue, in 'exploiting the ambiguous position of Aboriginal people as both inside and outside the constituted order, as citizens within and without the political community presupposed by the constitutional order' (2012: 535) the Embassy also effectively exposes the Australian state for mimicking the Aboriginal sovereignty it usurps. Here the traditional symbols of the diplomatic profession are creatively subverted for political ends.

Thus far we have explored how unofficial diplomacies have both developed new diplomatic skills and appropriated and mimicked traditional skills. This therefore supports the argument that, with the increasing pluralisation of diplomatic actors, 'old and new practices coexist in a mutually constitutive relationship' (Sending et al. 2015: 11; Cooper and Pouliot 2015). What, then, can this simultaneous diversification of diplomatic skills and knowledges and retention of traditional practices tell us about the nature of the interaction between state and non-state diplomats? For a start, it adds weight to assertions that we are not seeing the decline of state diplomacy per se, but rather the gradual reconfiguration of diplomatic strategies by all actors. As such, this fundamentally challenges the binary distinction between state and non-state diplomacy which is so prevalent in extant scholarship. Rather than perceiving diplomacy as consisting of a 'core', 'a state-centric sphere and a *closed system* regulated by diplomatic law which has the character of *lex specialis* constituting a separate sphere within public international law' and its 'soft shell', 'a broad sphere which features various actors involved in diplomatic interactions including NGOs, enterprises, regions, ethnic groups and so on' (Bátora and Hynek 2014: 7) with little traffic between them, we suggest that the lens of transprofessionalization allows us to focus on *partnerships* and *hybridities* between national diplomatic services and a plethora of other professional actors.

5 Conclusion: Diplomatic Partnerships, Hybrid Diplomacies

This paper is premised on the assertion that we should take the *profession* of diplomacy seriously, but that we should do so in ways that are more open, dynamic and interdisciplinary than both conventional historical accounts and many contemporary analyses suggest. It is notable that even among some critical approaches to global politics, such as an important recent collection examining the constitutive role of diplomacy in the making of world politics, it is 'by conceiving of it as a profession' that the editors seek to 'problematize the contours of what diplomacy is and is not' (Sending, Pouliot and Neumann 2015: 5). According to Sending et al 'what makes a diplomat is a claim to jurisdictional control over certain tasks that are sanctioned by the state and recognized in international law' (Ibid.). Quite rightly, they do not take these tasks as a given and acknowledge that they may not be limited to 'official diplomats'. Still the state-sanctioned tasks of *what makes one a diplomat and one's engagement diplomatic* define for them *the contours* within which diplomacy can be imagined. Whilst the editors are genuinely interested 'to theorize diplomacy as an emergent phenomenon whose form changes over time' (Sending et al. 2015: 6), it is the profession that provides the essential form and the yardstick that measures what changes. Diplomacy is thus 'defined, in the broadest possible terms, as a claim to represent a given polity to the outside world' (Ibid.).

But can this definition capture the richness and complexity of the diplomatic world before us? To be sure, definitions offer useful limits for ordering knowledge but also—even when they claim broadness—limitations on producing new knowledge. As Friedrich Nietzsche put it in *The Genealogy of Morals*: 'Only that which has no history can be defined' (1887/2012: 13). As we have discussed above, diplomacy certainly has a long history, preceding as well as following its weak and incomplete professionalization. That is why the replication of the 'professional', state-sanctioned tasks seriously limits our understanding of its practice. In the definition given by Sending et al, it does so in at least two ways.

First, besides the representation of a 'given polity', diplomacy can also entail *the representation of global causes and claimed service to humanity as a whole*. As discussed in the previous section, international NGO work, celebrity diplomacy and issue campaigning are good examples of advocating and missionizing for a wide range of 'good causes', such as poverty alleviation, asylum granting, children's rights, biodiversity and so on. An example of this concerns the adoption of the designation 'everyday ambassador', especially among the youth, which entails mastering and using communications tools 'to foster meaningful connections with others, whether inside our own communities or halfway around the world' (Otto 2015: kindle-lcn 201). Key to everyday ambassadorship is the building of meaningful and sustainable polities, domestic and foreign, and to that extent its range and scope can be global. Consider how the bulk of *everyday* diplomatic work is expended in single-issue advocacy, in *speaking for* something important and not necessarily in the *representation of* a single polity. It may be that through their everyday ambassadorship they implicitly seek to represent the cosmopolis, though the definition offered by Sending et al above, i.e. 'a claim to represent a given polity to the outside world' (2015: 5), seems to preclude this possibility as well.

Second, beyond representation of a 'given polity', it is important to remember that diplomacy can also entail the *mediation* work between polities as well as other estranged or conflicted entities. In other words, quite a large part of diplomatic work with regard to conflict resolution, third-party facilitation, local peacebuilding, and everyday in-betweenness seems a priori to be excluded from the diplomatic radar that only picks up 'professionals' representing and advancing the interests of polities. For example, for Richard Sennett, focusing on daily social encounters, diplomacy is precisely about building cooperation and togetherness. 'Everyday diplomacy' is 'the craft of working with people we disagree with, perhaps don't like, or don't understand.' (Sennett 2012: 31; cfr. Constantinou 2016). This type of 'non-professional' daily diplomacy is a reflexive way through which *dialogic* conversation is put into practice, exploring and experimenting with an open field of possibilities, rather than merely seeking to synthesize the preformed thesis-antithesis arguments of *dialectical* conversations.

On this point, authors like Rossow, reflecting on 'the professionalization of the new diplomacy', also start from a different basis than the idea of diplomacy as the representation of polities: 'Precisely, and quite simply, the professional service rendered by the diplomat is the minimizing of distortion and friction in cross-cultural communications and operations' (Rossow 1962: 563). For Rossow, there could be a 'variety of possible clients' and 'functional specialties' just as in any other profession:

> They [the diplomats] can serve as overseas business executives, journalists, technical advisers, negotiators, economic analysts, foreign traders, and so on. But it is the professional service in its cross-cultural context that is the unifying and defining theme of the profession, overriding differences in subspecialty and cliency.
>
> ROSSOW 1962: 563–4

In short, the diplomatic profession is turned on its head and is certainly not limited to the diplomatic corps or officially designated diplomats: it is rather located in the everyday, cross-cultural and interstitial space, and though it may certainly extend to the business of representing polities, this is not its core characteristic. For Rossow the professionalization of the 'new diplomacy' is quintessentially a transprofessionalization, although this is not a term he has used.

In this paper we have sought to expand upon and add conceptual and empirical nuance to Rossow's assertions by setting out three inter-linked approaches to understanding the relationship between diplomacy and professionalism. First, we traced how professionalization has been a long historical process which severed diplomacy from being a civic duty. In essence the professionalization of diplomacy entailed borrowing from different vocations—among others, notably, the clergy, the literati, the courtiers and the jurists—but this process has, certainly in comparison to other professions, been somewhat weak and incomplete. A strict vocational canon has not materialised through the professional diplomatic 'establishment'. Rather, for diplomacy, the main stamp of approval and legitimacy has been the authority of the sovereign state.

Second, we turned to ideas from the sociology of professions to examine the extent to which the professionalization of diplomacy can be understood as a process of functional differentiation of a particular, modern diplomatic system in the context of wider social systems of global modernity. We set out both how diplomacy has developed as a differentiated-distinguished profession which seeks to secure its autonomy and establish professional 'barriers' to entry, and how diplomacy is being de-differentiated through articulations with other professional cultures. The latter has been shaped by the structures of global governance that have required diplomacy to be a transnational vocation, and to establish alliances with other fields of expertise. As such, we have seen the increasing fragmentation of diplomatic activity, and the gradual erosion of the privileged monopoly of state diplomats whereby the barriers of entry to the profession are being broken down.

Third, in developing this idea of a paradox in the evolution of the diplomatic profession we expanded our gaze to look at the role of 'new' diplomatic actors, from NGOs and transnational corporations to de facto states and representatives from minority communities. We argued that the proliferation of these non-state actors seeking to practice diplomacy on the international stage has completely *trans*professionalized (not *de*professionalized) diplomacy. On the one hand, these non-state diplomats have brought new skills and knowledges to the table, from scientific and first hand expertise related to issue-based diplomacy to creative innovations in digital technology and sophisticated advocacy networking strategies. On the other hand, there has also been a strategic emulation of traditional diplomatic skills, with non-state actors seeking to learn the diplomatic game and claim legitimacy through mimicking formal diplomatic practices and undergoing socialization in the mores of traditional diplomatic culture. We argue that these trends of transprofessional diplomacy offer particular insights into the changing nature of state and non-state interactions in the diplomatic sphere. Nonetheless, an important predicament remains:

> Will (and should) nonstate entities be absorbed, coopted, and regulated by the norms and practices of the state system ...? ... Or will we move toward a world society (Buzan 2004) in which nonstate norms and practices reshape the state-based diplomatic culture, rendering it less state-centric, less hierarchical, less territorial, more transparent?
>
> WISEMAN 2011: 712

Rather than cooption of non-state diplomatic actors into the state system or complete transformation of the diplomatic realm, our analysis points to a situation of complex networking, intricate diplomatic partnerships and hybrid diplomacies.

By thinking through transprofessionalization we can see the relationship between diplomatic actors of different legal statuses and from different professional backgrounds not solely as conflictual or adversarial, as has commonly been the case in work on paradiplomacy (Aldecoa and Keating 1999) and on government/NGO interactions, but as potentially complementary and synergistic (Mamadouh and van der Wusten 2016; Cooper and Hocking 2000). Understanding these as dynamic *diplomatic partnerships* both refutes the assumption that diplomacy is a domain reserved for states and brings to the fore the complex and often contradictory situation of diplomatic relations. As Hocking notes, 'private actors may act as opponents of government, as agents and as comanagers within global policy networks' (2004: 152). There have been useful initial forays into charting the landscape of diplomatic partnerships, from Cooper and Hocking's (2000) notion of NGOs acting as a 'kick-starter' for diplomacy around particular issues, triggering coordinated advocacy by governments and civil society organizations, to Hocking's (2004) formulation of diplomats as 'boundary-spanners' between the domestic and the foreign. However, further empirical and conceptual analysis remains to be done. In particular, we suggest that attention needs to be paid to the dynamism, fluidity and contingency of diplomatic partnerships. As we have highlighted through our analysis of transprofessional diplomacy, it is crucial to acknowledge and analyse both how the legal and political status of diplomatic actors can morph over time and over space, and how power relations between diplomatic 'partners' are similarly malleable, with their characteristics shifting according to changing geopolitical imperatives.

One potentially productive framing is that of *hybrid diplomacies*. Embracing the fact that the 'line between official and unofficial forms of diplomacy is increasingly becoming blurred' (Betsill 2008: 205; Gregory 2016), the notion of hybridity allows us to see a multitude of different actors as both intertwined with each other and co-constitutive of the ongoing transformation of diplomatic practice. As Francesca Dickson notes:

> supranational institutions can act in ways previously reserved to states, as an arbiter of international force, for example, yet may not possess the representational qualities of states themselves. International NGOs or citizens' groups may legitimately represent the interests of constituent groups overlapping with those of states; yet not have the diplomatic authority or institutional capacity to convey these interests effectively.

> Such hybridity is significant in the sense that it opens up new diplomatic space, presenting alternative practices that operate under a different—perhaps less stringent—set of "rules".
>
> DICKSON 2014: 1

It is precisely these 'new diplomatic spaces' and 'alternative practices' that, we argue, the lens of transprofessionalization can shine a spotlight onto. Key to this is perceiving diplomatic partnerships and hybrid diplomacies in terms of both top-down and bottom-up practices of diplomacy. With regards to the latter, as noted above, the likes of everyday diplomacy can be practised in the context of a postmodern global polity not representing given polities and where established separations are constantly transgressed or become less relevant. As such, this challenges assumptions of a zero-sum game with regards to diplomacy, as well as Sharp's (2009) assertion that diplomacy only exists in conditions of separateness. Whilst exploring the dynamics of 'separation' vis-à-vis the diplomatic realm is beyond the scope of this paper, we suggest that transprofessional diplomacy opens up this core issue animating diplomatic studies in productive ways.

More generally, we propose that transprofessionalization has the potential to contribute both to how diplomacy is *studied*, and to how it is *practised*. As noted above, the 'profession' of diplomacy is consistently and problematically used in the study of diplomacy to determine *what is* or *can be* 'diplomacy'. The notion of transprofessionalization, by contrast, offers a more flexible and accommodating approach that acknowledges the expansion of diplomatic actors and spaces, embraces the possibilities of dynamic networks and relationships and the contested nature of the meaning of professionalism itself, and is open to new modes of being a diplomat in the world today.

To realize that diplomacy is in many respects fully transprofessionalized and in other respects still undergoing a process of transprofessionalization has important repercussions for the conventional understanding about how diplomacy can and should be studied. To embrace a broader, more open understanding of the diplomatic profession requires fostering dialogue between and across different schools of thought avoiding scholarly Manicheism. This will necessitate a greater engagement across a range of academic fields, beyond those traditionally cultivated in diplomatic studies, namely international law, diplomatic history and international relations. As noted in this paper, valuable insights and innovative methodologies can be drawn from work in sociology, political geography, social anthropology, communication or cultural studies amongst others. In turn, a nuanced interpretation of transprofessional diplomacy can contribute to understandings of other professions that are also undergoing important transformations, engaging their own modes of partnership and hybridity.

Finally, we suggest that transprofessional diplomacy is key to our understanding of how diplomacy is actually practised. Instead of professional solipsism being that which actually delivers positive results, it is the complementarity of skills, the adoption of flexible organisational structures, the fruitful combination of diverse types of knowledge, the cultivation of innovation and creativity, and the recognition of a multiplicity of actors and their competing legitimacies that drives diplomatic practice. By broadening our definitions of both 'professionals' and the 'diplomatic realm', we can be attentive to how the contact and exchange between the wide range of those individuals professing to act diplomatically, historically and contemporaneously, offers opportunities for mutual learning and fruitful collaboration. Indeed, these opportunities raise the question of whether diplomacy today is truly both an 'occasional' and 'professional' vocation. In narrow terms this means state-based diplomacy being more receptive to other forms of knowledge and professional skills that can, in turn enhance diplomatic practice. Rather than policy making being done in 'Cathedral mode'—written in-house by 'experts'—embracing transprofessionality opens up a diplomatic marketplace where information, strategies, expertise and skills from a diverse range of sectors can be engaged with. But, as we have argued in this paper, transprofessional diplomacy can potentially have more far reaching implications. Returning to arguments made by Robert Rossow on 'the professionalization of the new diplomacy' over fifty years ago, the notion of transprofessionalization opens up possibilities for creative thinking within diplomacy: a field which fundamentally 'deals in uncertainties, and recognizes the openness of the world to change' (Dingwall and King 1995: 18).

List of References

Abbas, J. A. (2009). 'Managers and Diplomacy', *International Journal of Commerce & Management*, 19(4): 256–259.

Abbott, A. (1988). *The System of Professions: An Essay on the Division of Expert Labor*. Chicago: University of Chicago Press.

Acuto, M. (2013). *Global Cities, Governance and Diplomacy: The Urban Link*. London: Routledge.

Adler-Nissen, R. (2013). 'State nobility and the invention of a new social group' in Kauppi, Niilo and Mikael Rask Madsen (eds.) *Transnational Power Elites: The New Professionals of Governance, Law and Security*, New York: Routledge, pp. 65–80.

Aeschines (2005). *On the False Embassy*. G. Greaney (ed.). Lewiston: Edwin Mellen.

Aldecoa, F. and M. Keating, Eds. (1999). *Paradiplomacy in Action: The Foreign Relations of Subnational Governments*. Portland: Frank Cass.

Amann, W., S. Khan, O. Salzmann, U. Steger and A. Ionescu-Somers (2011). 'Managing external pressures through corporate diplomacy', *Journal of General Management*, 33(1): 33–49.

Anand, D. (2007). *Geopolitical Exotica: Tibet in Western Imagination.* Minneapolis: Unversity of Minnesota Press.

Auer, M. (1998). 'Colleagues or Combatants? Experts as Environmental Diplomats', *International Negotiation*, 3(2): 267–287.

Badie, B. (2008). *Le diplomat et l' intrus: l'entrée des societies dans l' arène international.* Paris: Fayard.

Bagger, T. (2015). '"Review2014": A project of reflection and change in German Foreign Policy', *The Hague Journal of Diplomacy*, 10(4): 421–429.

Bailes, A. K. (2004). 'Reflections on thirty years in the Diplomatic Service'. *Contemporary British History*, 18(3): 189–197.

Balfour, R., C. Carta and K. Raik, Eds. (2015). *The European External Action Service and National Diplomacies: From Complementarity to Convergence?* Farnham: Ashgate.

Bátora, J. (2005). 'Does the European Union transform the institution of diplomacy?' *Journal of European Public Policy*, 12(1): 44–66.

Bátora, J. (2013). The 'Mitrailleuse Effect': The EEAS as an interstitial organization and the dynamics of innovation in diplomacy. *Journal of Common Market Studies*, 51(4): 598–613.

Batora, J. and N. Hynek (2014). *Fringe Players and the Diplomatic Order: The New Heteronomy*. Basingtoke: Palgrave-Macmillan.

Bazouni Y. (2005). *Le métier de diplomate*, Paris: L'Harmattan.

Bazzoli, M. (2002). 'Ragion di stato e interesse degli stati. La trattatistica sull'ambasciatore dal XV al XVIII secolo', *Nuova Rivista Storica*, 86: 283–328.

Behr, H. (2010). *A history of international political theory: ontologies of the international.* Basingtoke: Palgrave-Macmillan.

Behrens, B. (1936). 'Treatises on the ambassador written in the fifteenth and Early sixteenth centuries.' *English Historical Review*, 51: 616–627.

Beier, J. M. (2007). 'Introduction: Indigenous diplomacies.' *Canadian Foreign Policy Journal*, 13(3): 9–11.

Beier, J. M., Ed. (2010). *Indigenous Diplomacies*. Basingstoke: Palgrave-Macmillan.

Benson, D. R. and R. K. Kjelgren (2014). 'Tacit Diplomacy in Life Sciences: A Foundation for Science Diplomacy'. *Science and Diplomacy*, 3(1): 1–9.

Berger, C., M. Humuza and S. Janssens (2013). *Training in the EEAS: How to Live-Up to the Potentials of the Lisbon Treaty*, Berlin: SWP Working Paper.

Berridge, G. R., M. Keens-Soper, and T. G. Otte (2001). *Diplomatic Theory from Machiavelli to Kissinger*: Basingstoke: Palgrave.

Betsill, M. M. (2008). 'Reflections on the analytical framework and NGO diplomacy'. *NGO diplomacy: the influence of nongovernmental organizations in international environmental negotiations*. M. M. Betsill and E. Corell. Cambridge, MA: MIT Press: 177–206.

Betsill, M. M. and E. Corell (2008). 'Introduction to NGO diplomacy', in M. M. Betsil and E. Corell (eds.), *NGO diplomacy: the influence of nongovernmental organizations in international environmental negotiations*. Cambridge, MA: MIT Press: 1–17.

Betsill, M. M. and E. Corell, Eds. (2008). *NGO diplomacy: the influence of nongovernmental organizations in international environmental negotiations*. Cambridge, MA: MIT Press.

Bhabha, H. (1984). 'Of Mimicry and Man: The Ambivalence of Colonial Discourse.' *Discipleship: A Special Issue on Psychoanalysis*, 28: 125–133.

Biow, D. (2002). *Doctors, Ambassadors, Secretaries: Humanism and Professions in Renaissance Italy*. Chicago: Chicago University Press.

Bjola, C. and M. Holmes, Eds. (2015). *Digital Diplomacy: theory and practice*. London: Routledge.

Black, J. (2010). *A history of diplomacy*. London: Reaktion Books.

Bob, C. (2005). *The Marketing of Rebellion: Insurgents, Media, and International Activism*. Cambridge: Cambridge University Press.

Bourdieu, P. (1977). *Outline of a Theory of Practice*. Cambridge: Cambridge University Press.

Bowd, S. D. (2000). 'The Republic of Ideas: Venice, Florence and the Defence of Liberty 1525–1530'. *History*, 85: 404–427.

Brante, T. (2010). 'Professional Fields and Truth Regimes: In Search of Alternative Approaches.' *Current Sociology*, 9(61): 843–886.

Bull, H. (1977/2002). *The Anarchical Society*. London, Macmillan Press.

Castiglione, B. (1528/1967). *The Book of the Courtier*. London: Penguin.

Carpenter, C. (2011). 'Vetting the Advocacy Agenda: Network Centrality and the Paradox of Weapons Norms.' *International Organization*, 65(1): 69–102.

Carta, C. (2012). *The European Union Diplomatic Service: Ideas, Preferences and Identities*. London: Routledge.

Chong, A. and J. Troy (2011). 'A Universal Sacred Mission and the Universal Secular Organization: The Holy See and the United Nations.' *Politics, Religion & Ideology*, 12(3): 335–354.

Clark, A. M. (2001). *Diplomacy of conscience: Amnesty International and changing human rights norms*. Princeton: Princeton University Press.

Constantinou, C. M. (1996). *On the way to diplomacy*. Minneapolis: University of Minnesota Press.

Constantinou, C. M. (2006). 'On homo-diplomacy'. *Space and Culture*, 9(4): 351–364.

Constantinou, C. M. and J. Der Derian, Eds. (2010). *Sustainable Diplomacies*. London: Palgrave-Macmillan.

Constantinou, C. M. (2013). 'Between Statecraft and Humanism: Diplomacy and Its Forms of Knowledge'. *International Studies Review*, 15(2): 141–162.

Constantinou, C. M. (2016). 'Everyday diplomacy: mission, spectacle and the remaking of diplomatic culture', in Dittmer, J. and McConnell, F. (eds.) *Diplomatic Cultures and International Politics: Translations, Spaces and Alternatives*, Abingdon: Routledge: 23–40.

Constantinou, C. M., P. Kerr and P. Sharp, Eds. (2016). *The SAGE Handbook of Diplomacy*. London: Sage.

Constantinou, C. M. and Opondo, S. O. (2016). 'Engaging the 'Ungoverned': The Merging of Diplomacy, Defence and Development'. *Cooperation and Conflict*, 51(3): 307–324.

Cooper, A. F. (2008). *Celebrity diplomacy*. London: Paradigm Publishers.

Cooper, A. F. and Hocking, B. (2000). 'Governments, Non-Governmental Organizations and the Re-Calibration of Diplomacy'. *Global Society*, 14: 361–376.

Cooper, A. F., B. Hocking, W. Maley (2008). *Global governance and diplomacy: worlds apart?* Basingstoke: Palgrave-Macmillan.

Cooper, A. F. and V. Pouliot (2015). 'How much is global governance changing?: The G20 as international practice.' *Cooperation and Conflict*, 50(3): 334–350.

Copeland, D. (2009). *Guerrilla diplomacy: rethinking international relations*. Boulder: Lynne Rienner Publishers.

Corell, E. and M. M. Betsill (2008). 'Analytical Framework: assessing the influence of NGO diplomats', in M. M. Betsill and E. Corell (eds.), *NGO diplomacy: the influence of nongovernmental organizations in international environmental negotiations*. Cambridge, MA: MIT Press: 19–42.

Cornago, N. (2010). 'On the Normalization of Sub-State Diplomacy.' *The Hague Journal of Diplomacy*, 5: 11–36.

Cornago, N. (2013). *Plural Diplomacies: Normative Predicaments and Functional Imperatives*. Leiden: Brill.

Cornago, N. (2016). '(Para) diplomatic cultures: old and new,' in J. Dittmer and F. McConnell (eds.), *Diplomatic Cultures and International Politics: Translations, Spaces and Alternatives*. Abingdon: Routledge: 175–194.

Cornago, N. (2016). 'Diplomatic Knowledge' in Constantinou C. M., Kerr, P. and Sharp, P., (eds.), *The SAGE Handbook of Diplomacy*. London: Sage: 133–146.

Corrie, K. L. (2015). 'The International Criminal Court: using technology in network diplomacy,' in C. Bjola and M. Holmes, *Digital Diplomacy: Theory and Practice*. London: Routledge: 145–163.

Craig, G. A. (1952). 'The Professional Diplomat and His Problems, 1919–1939.' *World Politics*, 4(2): 145–158.

Cross, M. and J. Melissen. 2013. *Public Diplomacy in Europe: Soft Power at Work*. New York: Palgrave Macmillan.

De Callières, F. (1983). *The Art of Diplomacy*. Edited by Keens-Soper, H. M. A. and Schweizer, K. W. New York: Holmes & Meier.

De Raymond, J. F. (2015). *L'Esprit de la diplomatie: Du particulier à l'universel*. Paris: Manitoba-Les Belles Lettres.

Demosthenes (2000). *On the False Embassy*. MacDowell D. M. (ed.). Oxford: Oxford University Press.

Denéchère, Y., Ed. (2004). *Femmes et diplomatie: France, XXe siècle*. Berlin: Peter Lang.

Dent, M. and S. Whitehead, Eds. (2002). *Managing Professional Identities: Knowledge, performativity and the 'new' professional*. London: Routledge.

Denza, E. (2016). *Diplomatic Law: Commentary of the Vienna Convention on Diplomatic Relations*, (4th Edition) Oxford: Oxford University Press.

Der Derian, J. (1987). *On Diplomacy: A Genealogy of Western Estrangement*. Oxford: Blackwell.

Devin, G., and M. Toernquist-Chesnier (2010). 'Burst diplomacy. The diplomacies of foreign policy: actors and methods.' *Brazilian Political Science Review*, 4(2): 60–77.

Dezalay, Y. (2004). 'Les Courtiers de l'international: Heritiers Cosmopolites, Mercenaires de l'imperialisme et Missionnaires de l'universel'. *Actes de la Recherche en Sciences Sociales*, 151–152: 5–34.

Dickson, F. (2014). *Sub-state Governments as Diplomatic Actors: The Good, the Bad and the Ugly*. The Diplomacy of Monsters workshop. Cardiff University. 29–30 May 2014.

Dingwall, R. (1999). 'Professions and social order in a global society.' *International Review of Sociology*, 9(1): 131–140.

Dingwall, R. and M. D. King (1995). 'Herbert Spencer and the Professions: Occupational Ecology Reconsidered', *Sociological Theory*, 13(1): 14–24.

Dittmer, J. and F. McConnell, Eds. (2016). *Diplomatic Cultures and International Politics: Translations, Spaces and Alternatives*. Abingdon: Routledge.

Dizard, W. P. (2001). *Digital diplomacy: U.S. foreign policy in the information age*. Westport, CT: Praeger.

Duke, S. (2012). 'Diplomatic Training and the Challenges Facing the EEAS'. *The Hague Journal of Diplomacy*, 7(1): 95–114.

Dutch Advisory Committee on Modernising the Diplomatic Service (2013). *Modernising Dutch Diplomacy: Progress report*, Amsterdam: Ministry of Foreign Affairs.

Duyvendak, J. W., T. Knijn and M. Kremer, Eds. (2005). *Policy, People, and the New Professional: De-Professionalisation and Re-Professionalisation in Care and Welfare*, Amsterdam: Amsterdam University Press.

Evetts, J. (2013). 'Professionalism: Value and Ideology', *Current Sociology*, 61(5): 5–6.

Faulconbridge, J. R. and D. Muzio (2012). 'Professions in a Globalizing World: Towards a transnational sociology of the professions', *International Sociology*, 27(1): 136–152.

FCO (2016). *Future FCO Report*, London: FCO.

Finnemore, M. and K. Sikkink (1998). 'International norm dynamics and political change.' *International Organization*, 52: 887–917.

Fletcher, T. (2016). *Naked Diplomacy: Power and Statecraft on the Digital Age*. London: William Collins.

Foley, G., A. Schaap, and E. Howell, Eds. (2013). *The Aboriginal Tent Embassy: Sovereignty, Black Power, Land Rights and the State*. Abingdon: Routledge.

Fourcade, M. (2006). 'The construction of a global profession: The transnationalization of economics.' *American Journal of Sociology*, 112(1): 145–194.

Frey, L., and Frey, M. (1999). *The History of Diplomatic Immunity*. Ohio State University Press.

Freeman, C. W. (1995). 'Diplomacy as a Profession' Remarks to the American Foreign Service Association, available http://chasfreeman.net/diplomacy-as-a-profession.

Gabrielyan, V., P. Stroobants and E. Berg (2016). 'How do you tailor diplomatic training? Sizing up peer institutions and their training practices for the Diplomatic School of Armenia'. *Global Affairs*, 2(2): 223–231.

Gerbaudo, P. and M. Pianta (2012). 'Twenty years of global civil society events: The rise and fall of Parallel Summits, the novelty of global days of action', in M. Kaldor, H. L. Moore and S. Selchow (eds.) *Global Society 2012: Ten Years of Critical Reflections*. Basingtoke: Palgrave: 190–193.

Gheciu, A. (2005). *NATO in the 'New Europe'*. Berkeley: Stanford University Press.

Gill, S. (2012). 'Towards a Radical Concept of Praxis: Imperial "common sense" versus the Post-modern Prince.' *Millennium*, 40(3): 505–524.

Gregory, B. (2016). 'Mapping boundaries in diplomacy's public dimension.' *The Hague Journal of Diplomacy*, 11(1): 1–25.

Guedes, A. M. (2008). *Raising Diplomats: Political, genealogical and administrative constraints on patterns of training for diplomacy*. Vienna: Diplomatic Academy of Vienna.

Haas, P. (1992). 'Epistemic Communities and International Policy Coordination: Introduction.' *International Organization*, 46(1): 1–35.

Hackspiel-Mikosch, E. (2005). 'Uniforms, diplomatic', Valerie Steele (ed.) *Encyclopedia of Clothing and Fashion*, vol. 3, New York: Thomson Gale: 362–364.

Hamilton, K. and R. Langhorne (1995). *The Practice of Diplomacy: its evolution, theory and administration*. London: Routledge.

Harr, J. E. (1969). *The Professional Diplomat*. Princeton: Princeton University Press.

Harrington, B. (2015). 'Going global: professionals and the micro-foundations of institutional change'. *Journal of Professions and Organization*, 2: 103–121.

Hedges, H. (2010). 'Blurring the boundaries: Connecting research, practice and professional learning'. *Cambridge Journal of Education*, 40(3): 299–314.

Heine, J. (2008). 'On the Manner of Practising the New Diplomacy', in A. F. Cooper, B. Hocking, and W. Maley (eds.) *Global Governance and Diplomacy: Worlds Apart?*, Houndmills: Palgrave-Macmillan: 271–287.

Henrikson, A. K. (1999). 'Diplomacy: Profession in Peril?' in C. Jennings and N. Hopkinson (eds.), *Current Issues in International Diplomacy and Foreign Policy*, vol. 1, London: The Stationary Office: 3–47.

Hocking, B. (1999). 'Patrolling the 'Frontier: Globalization, Localization and the 'Actorness' of Non-Central Governments.' *Regional and Federal Studies*, 9(1): 17–39.

Hocking, B. (2004). 'Privatizing Diplomacy?', *International Studies Perspectives*, 5(2): 147–152.

Hocking, B., J. Melissen, S. Riordan and Paul Sharp (2012). *Futures for Diplomacy: Integrative Diplomacy for the 21st Century*. The Hague: Clingendael.

Hormats, R. D. (2012). 'Science diplomacy and twenty-first century statecraft.' *Science & Diplomacy*, 1.

Hulme, R., D. Cracknell and A. Owens (2009). 'Learning in third spaces: developing transprofessional understanding through practitioner enquiry.' *Educational Action Research*, 17(4): 537–550.

Iveson, K. (2013). 'The spatial politics of the Aboriginal Tent Embassy, Canberra', in G. Foley, A. Schaap and E. Howell (eds.), *The Aboriginal Tent Embassy: Sovereignty, Black Power, Land Rights and the State*. Abingdon: Routledge: 251–266.

Jazbec, M. (2013). 'The sociology of Diplomacy: A general outline with some aspects and dilemmas'. *Perspectives*, 21(1): 87–108.

Jayasuriya, K. (2004). 'The new regulatory state and relational capacity'. *Policy & Politics*, 32(4), 487–501.

Jayasuriya, K. (2005). 'Breaking the Westphalian frame: regulatory State, fragmentation and diplomacy', in J. Robertson and M. East (eds.), *Diplomacy and Developing Nations: post-Cold-War foreign policy-making structures and processes*. London: Routledge: 39–54.

Juncos, A. E. and K. Pomorska (2014). 'Manufacturing Esprit de Corps: The Case of the European External Action Service'. *Journal of Common Market Studies*, 52(2): 302–319.

Kauppi, N. and M. R. Madsen (2014). 'Fields of Global Governance: How Transnational Power Elites Can Make Global Governance Intelligible'. *International Political Sociology*, 8(3): 324–330.

Keating, M. (1999). 'Regions and International Affairs: Motives, Opportunities and Strategies,' in F. Aldecoa and M. Keating (eds.), *Paradiplomacy in Action: The Foreign Relations of Subnational Governments*. Portland: Frank Cass: 1–16.

Keck, M. E. and K. Sikkink (1998). *Activists beyond borders*. Ithaca, Cornell University Press.

Keens-Soper (1983). 'The French Political Academy, 1712: A School of Ambassadors', artilve originally published in European Studies Review, reprinted in De Callières, F. (1983) *The Art of Diplomacy*. Edited by Keens-Soper, H. M. A. and Schweizer, K. W. New York: Holmes & Meier, pp. 189–218.

Kennan, G. (1997). 'Diplomacy without Diplomats', *Foreign Affairs*, vol. 76: 198–212.

Kennan, G. (2015). 'Diplomacy as a Profession', *Foreign Service Journal*. July–August.
Kerr, P. and G. Wiseman, Eds. (2013). *Diplomacy in a Globalizing World: Theories and Practices*, Oxford: Oxford University Press.
Kessler, M. Ch. (2012). *Les Ambassadeurs*, Paris, Presses de Sciences Po.
Kingston de Leusse, M. (1988). *Diplomate: une sociologie des ambassadeurs*. Paris: L'Harmattan.
Kissinger, H. (1994). *Diplomacy*. New York: Simon & Schuster.
Kleistra, Y. and N. Van Willigen (2010). 'Evaluating Diplomacy: A mission Impossible?' *Evaluation*, 16(2): 119–135.
Kopp, H. W. and C. A. Gillespie (2011). *Career Diplomacy: Life and Work in the US Foreign Service*. Washington DC: Georgetown University Press.
Kurbalija, J. and H. Slavik, Eds. (2001). *Language and Diplomacy*. Valetta: Diplo Foundation.
Kuus, M. (2014). *Geopolitics and Expertise: Knowledge and Authority in European Diplomacy*. London: Wiley.
Kuus, M. (2016). 'Diplomacy and audit: Technologies of knowledge in Europe', *Geoforum*, 68: 39–47.
Kuznetsov, A. (2014). *Theory and Practice of Paradiplomacy*. New York: Routledge.
Lacey, A. and S. Ilcan (2006). 'Voluntary Labor, Responsible Citizenship and International NGOs', *International Journal of Comparative Sociology*, 47(1): 34–53.
Lagon, M. and S. Grewoski (2015). 'Power to the People: Taking Diplomacy to the Streets', *The National Interest*, February 26th: 35.
Lancaster, C. (2008). *Foreign aid: Diplomacy, development, domestic politics*. Chicago: University of Chicago Press.
Langhorne, R. (1997). Current developments in diplomacy: Who are the diplomats now?, *Diplomacy & Statecraft*, 8(2): 1–15.
Larson, M. S. (1977). *The Rise of Professionalism: a Sociological Analysis*. Berkeley: University of California Press.
Leira, H. (2016). 'A Conceptual History of Diplomacy', in Constantinou, C. M., Kerr, P. and Sharp, P., (eds.), *The SAGE Handbook of Diplomacy*. London: Sage: 28–38.
Lemoine, J. (1995). *The International Civil Servant: An Endangered Species*. Leiden: Martinus-Nijhoff.
Lequesne Ch. and J. Heilbronn (2012). 'Senior Diplomats in the French Ministry of Foreign Affairs, When an Entrance Exam Still Determines the Career', *The Hague Journal of Diplomacy*, 7(3): 269–285.
London, M. (1999). *Principled leadership and Business Diplomacy: values-based strategies for management development*. London: Quorum-Greenwood.
Loriol, M. (2009). 'La carrière des diplomates français: entre parcours individuel et structuration collective'. *Sociologies*, on line: http://sociologies.revues.org/2936.

Loriol, M., F. Piotet, V. Boussard, and V. Porteret (2007). *Recherche en sociologie du travail sur les métiers diplomatiques*. Paris: Laboratoire Georges-Friedmann (CNRS / Paris I.

MAEDI (2015). *Une diplomatie globale por le XXIè siecle*. Paris: MAEDI.

Mamadouh, V. and H. van der Wusten (2016). 'The paradiplomacy of cities and regions: transnational relations between sub-state political entities' in Dittmer, J. and McConnell, F. (eds.) *Diplomatic Cultures and International Politics: Translations, Spaces and Alternatives*. Abingdon: Routledge: 135–153.

Marques Guedes, A. (2008). *Raising Diplomats. Political, genealogical and administrative constraints in training for diplomacy*. Vienna: Favorita Series-Diplomatiche Akademie.

Mastenbroek, W. (1999). 'Negotiating as emotion management.' *Theory, culture & society*, 16(4), 49–73.

Mattingly, G. (1988) *Renaissance Diplomacy*. New York: Dover Publications.

McConnell, F. (2016). *Rehearsing the State: The Political Practices of the Tibetan Government-in-Exile*. Oxford: Wiley Blackwell.

McConnell, F. (forthcoming). 'Liminal geopolitics: the subjectivity and spatiality of diplomacy at the margins', *Transactions of the Institute of British Geographers*. doi: 10.1111/tran.12156

McConnell, F., T. Moreau, and J. Dittmer (2012). 'Mimicking state diplomacy: The legitimizing strategies of unofficial diplomacies'. *Geoforum*, 43(4): 804–814.

Megahed, N., B. Van der Heijden, M. Shaker and K. Wahba (2012). 'A Framework for Developing a Multiple-Jobs Competency Model for Diplomats', *International Journal of Business and Social Science*, 3(24).

Megoran, N. (2010). 'Towards a geography of peace: pacific geopolitics and evangelical Christian Crusade apologies.' *Transactions of the Institute of British Geographers* 35(3): 382–398.

Melissen, J. and Y. Sohn (2015). *Understanding Public Diplomacy in East Asia: Middle Power Democracies and Emerging Powers in a Turbulent Region*. New York: Palgrave-Macmillan.

Melissen, J. (2005). *The new public diplomacy: soft power in international relations*. Basingstoke: Palgrave-Macmillan.

Mösslang, M., and T. Riotte (2008). *The diplomats' world: a cultural history of diplomacy, 1815–1914*. Oxford: Oxford University Press.

Muldoon, J. P. (2005). 'The Diplomacy of Business', *Diplomacy and Statecraft*, 16(3): 341–359.

Muldoon, P. and A. Schaap (2012). 'Aboriginal Sovereignty and the Politics of Reconciliation: The Constituent Power of the Aboriginal Embassy in Australia.' *Environment and Planning D: Society and Space*, 30(3): 534–550.

Murdoch, Z. and B. Geys (2014). 'Institutional Dynamics in International Organizations: Lessons from the Recruitment Procedures of the European External Action Service', *Organization Studies*, 35(12): 1793–1811.

Murray, C. (2006). *Murder in Samarkand: a British ambassador's controversial defiance of tyranny in the war on terror*. London: Mainstream Publishing.

Neumann, I. B. (2005). 'To Be a Diplomat', *International Studies Perspectives*, 6: 72–93.

Neumann, I. B. (2012). *At Home with Diplomats: Inside a European Foreign Ministry*. Ithaca: Cornell University Press.

Neumann, I. B. 'Globalization and Diplomacy', in A. F. Cooper, B. Hocking, and W. Maley (eds.), *Global Governance and Diplomacy: Worlds Apart?*, Houndmills: Palgrave-Macmillan.

Nicolson, H. (1939). *Curzon, The Last Phase, 1919–1925: A Study in Post-War Diplomacy*. New York: Harcourt Brace and Co.

Nicolson, H. (1954). *The evolution of diplomatic method*. London: Constable.

Niedner-Kalthoff, U. (2005) *Ständige Vertretung: Eine Ethnographie diplomatischer Lebenswelten*. Berlin: Transcript Verlag.

Niedner-Kalthoff, U. (2006). 'Rotation und Objektivität. Diplomaten als transnationale Migranten', in F. Kreutzer and S. Roth (eds.), *Transnationale Karrieren*. Berlin: Springer: 83–99.

Nietzsche, F. (2010). *On the genealogy of morals and ecce homo*. New York: Vintage.

Nowony, T. (2011). *Diplomacy and global governance: the diplomatic service in an age of worldwide interdependence*. New York: Transaction Publishers.

Numelin, R. J. (1950). *The beginnings of diplomacy: a sociological study of intertribal and international relations*. Oxford: Oxford University Press.

Nybø, G. (2004). 'Personnel Development for Dissolving Jobs: Towards a Competency-Based Approach.' *The International Journal of Human Resource Management*, 15(3): 549–564.

Oglesby, D. M. (2016). 'Diplomatic Language', in Constantinou, C. M., Kerr, P. and Sharp, P. (eds.), *The SAGE Handbook of Diplomacy*, London: Sage: 242–254.

Opondo, S. O. (2016). 'Diplomacy and the Colonial Encounter', in Constantinou C. M., Kerr, P. and Sharp, P. (eds.), *The SAGE Handbook of Diplomacy*. London: Sage: 39–53.

Ordeix-Rigo, E. and J. Duarte (2009). 'From Public Diplomacy to Corporate Diplomacy: Increasing Corporation's Legitimacy and Influence', *American Behavioral Scientist*, 53: 549–564.

Otto, K. (2015). *Everyday Ambassador: Make a Difference by Connecting in a Disconnected World*. New York: Atria.

Pecquet, A. (1737/2004). Discours sur L'Art de Negocier, extracts of which are published in G. R. Berridge (ed.), 2004, *Diplomatic Classics*, Houndmills: Palgrave-Macmillan: 159–173.

Poulliot, V. and J. Cornut (2015). 'Practice theory and the study of diplomacy: A research agenda.' *Cooperation and Conflict*, 50(3): 297–315.

Queller, Donald E. (1967). *The Office of Ambassador in the Middle Ages*. Princeton, NJ: Princeton University Press.

Richelieu, A. J. D. P. (1961). *The Political Testament of Cardinal Richelieu*. Madison: University of Wisconsin Press.

Princen, T. (1994). *Environmental NGOs in world politics: Linking the local and the global*. London: Routledge.

QDDR (2010). Rodham Clinton, H. *The First Quadrennial Diplomacy and Development Review: Leading Through Civilian Power.* Washington DC: US Department of State.

Rana, K. S. (2013). *The Contemporary Embassy: Paths to Diplomatic Excellence*. Basingstoke: Palgrave Macmillan.

Riordan, S. (2002). *The new diplomacy*. Cambridge: Polity.

Roberts, I. (2010). *The Development of Modern Diplomacy*. London: Chatham House.

Ross, C. (2007). *Independent diplomat: dispatches from an unaccountable elite*. Ithaca: Cornell University Press.

Rossow, R. (1962). 'The professionalization of the new diplomacy', *World Politics*, 14(4): 561–575.

Saner, R. and L. Yiu (2000). 'The need for business diplomats, entrepreneurial politicians and cultural ambassadors', in W. Kraus and P. Trappe (eds.), *Social Strategies*, Berne: Peter Lang: 411–28.

Saner, R., L. Yiu and M. Sondegaard (2000). 'Business diplomacy management: a core competency for global companies', *Academy of Management Executive*, 14(1), 80–92.

Satow, S. E. (Lord Gore-Booth, ed.) ([1917] 1979). *Satow's Guide to Diplomatic Practice*, London: Longman.

Schäferhoff, M., S. Campe, and C. Kaan (2009). Transnational Public-Private Partnerships in International Relations: Making Sense of Concepts, Research Frameworks, and Results. *International Studies Review*, 11(3): 451–474.

Schweizer, K. (2011). 'François de Callières and the Marquis de Torcy's "Political Academy": New Evidence', *Canadian Journal of History*, 46(3): 619–625.

Seabrooke, L. (2014). 'Epistemic arbitrage: Transnational professional knowledge in action', *Journal of Professions and Organization*, 1(1): 49–64.

Seabrooke, L. (2015). 'Diplomacy as economic consultancy', in O. J. Sending, V. Pouliot and I. B. Neumann (eds.), *Diplomacy and the Making of World Politics*. Cambridge: Cambridge University Press: 195–219.

Sending, O. J., V. Pouliot, and I. B. Neumann (2011). 'The future of diplomacy: Changing practices, evolving relationships.' *International Journal*. 66(3): 527–542.

Sending, O. J., V. Pouliot, and I. B. Neumann, Eds. (2015). *Diplomacy and the Making of World Politics*. Cambridge: Cambridge University Press.

Sennett, R. (2012). *Together: The Rituals, Pleasures and Politics of Cooperation*. New Haven: Yale University Press.

Shadian, J. (2016). 'Not seeing like a state: Inuit diplomacies meet state sovereignty', in J. Dittmer and F. McConnell (eds.). *Diplomatic Cultures and International Politics: Translations, Spaces and Alternatives*, Abingdon Routledge: 153–174.

Sharp, P. (2009). *Diplomatic Theory of International Relations*. Cambridge: Cambridge University Press.

Sharp, P. (2012). *Diplomatic Theory of International Relations*. Cambridge: Cambridge University Press.

Sharp, P. and G. Wiseman, Eds. (2007). *The Diplomatic Corps as an Institution of International Society*. Basingstoke: Palgrave.

Sharp, P. (1997). 'Who needs diplomats? The Problem of Diplomatic Representation', *International Journal*, 52(4): 609–634.

Sluga, G. and C. James, Eds. (2015). *Women, Diplomacy and International Politics Since 1500*. New York: Routledge.

Sofer, S. (2013). *Courtiers of Civilization, The: A Study of Diplomacy*. New York: SUNY Press.

Sofer, S. (2007). 'The Diplomatic Corps as a Symbol of Diplomatic Culture', in P. Sharp and G. Wiseman (eds.) *The Diplomatic Corps as an Institution of International Society*. Houndmills: Palgrave-Macmillan: 31–38.

Steger, U. (2003). *Corporate Diplomacy: The Strategy for a Volatile, Fragmented Business Environment*. Sussex: John Wiley & Sons.

Tornquist-Chesnier, M. (2007). 'How the International Criminal Court came to life: The role of Non-Governmental Organisations.' *Global Society*, 21(3): 44–65.

Torstendahl, R. and M. Burrage, Eds. (1990). *The Formation of Professions: Knowledge, State and Strategy*. London: Sage.

Towns, A. and B. Niklasson (2016). Gender, International Status, and Ambassador Appointments. *Foreign Policy Analysis*, pre-print.

Trice, R., M. Hasegawa, and M. Kearns, Eds. (1995). *Corporate Diplomacy: Principled Leadership for the Global Community*. Washington DC: Center for Strategic and International Studies.

Turner, V. (1969). *The Ritual Process: Structure and Anti-structure*. Chicago, Aldine.

Van Leeuwen, D. (2013). Modernising Dutch diplomacy [Available from http://www.government.nl/documents-and-publications/reports/2014/05/22/final-report-modernising-diplomatic-service-by-docters-van-leeuwen.html.

Villar, C. (2011). *Le discours diplomatique*. Paris: L' Harmattan.

Watson, A. (1984). *Diplomacy: the dialogue between states*. London: Methuen.

Weber, M. (1991). *From Max Weber: essays in sociology*. London: Routledge.

White, H. C. (2008). *Identity & Control: How Social Formations Emerge*. Princeton: Princeton University Press.

Wigell, M. (2013). "The Aland Example as Norm Entrepreneurship." *International Journal on Minority and Group Rights*. 20: 67–84.

Wicquefort, A. (1681/2004). 'The Embassador and his Functions', extracts published in Berridge, G., *Diplomatic classics: selected texts from Commynes to Vattel*. Palgrave-Macmillan: 122–137.

Wilson, A. and F. McConnell (2015). 'Constructing legitimacy without legality in long term exile: Comparing Western Sahara and Tibet' *Geoforum*, 66: 203–214.

Wiseman, G. (2005). 'Pax Americana: Bumping into Diplomatic Culture', *International Studies Perspectives* 6(4): 409–430.

Wiseman, G. (2011). Bringing Diplomacy Back In: Time for Theory to Catch Up with Practice. *International Studies Review* 13: 710–3.

Wiseman, G., Ed. (2015). *Isolate or Engage: Adversarial States, US Foreign Policy, and Public Diplomacy*. Stanford: Stanford University Press.

www.ingramcontent.com/pod-product-compliance
Lightning Source LLC
Chambersburg PA
CBHW031333230926
51848CB00001B/223
9789004340442